Anger and Rage Addiction & the Self-Pact
New Lights on an Old Nemesis

Also by Stephen Rich Merriman, Ph.D.

When You Lose What You Can't Live Without
Outside Time: My Friendship with Wilbur
The Living Oracle: Wisdom & Divination for Everyday Life
Who's At Home In Your Body (When You're Not)?
Pathfinding Through Multiple Personality

Book and cover design by Tim Kinnel, *www.wordsareimages.com*
Cover photograph by Zacarias da Mata, fotolia.com

ISBN 978-0-9817698-5-1
Library of Congress Control Number: 2013942459
Library of Congress subject headings:
1. Anger—Treatment. 2. Aggression—Psychology
3. Mind-Body Relations, Metaphysics.
4. SELF-HELP/Anger Management
5. Self-help techniques. 6. Self-realization

Dear Joe,
Many blessings
and best wishes
to you.
— Stephen Rich Merriman

Septbe 6, '19

Anger and Rage Addiction
&
the Self-Pact

New Lights on an Old Nemesis

Stephen Rich Merriman, Ph.D.

Anger and Rage Addiction & The Self-Pact:
New Lights on an Old Nemesis

... is dedicated to Dr. Peter Conrad, a Boston-area psychiatrist who, in an informal group setting in the early 1970s, posed, in the form of an admonition, a single, simple riddle. This riddle caught my attention—and took me nearly forty years to fully comprehend, and then *solve*, in a manner that quite possibly he hadn't considered. I now, gratefully, reside in the riddle's solution.

Acknowledgements

I wish to acknowledge (by first name only, for understandable reasons), those who have engaged in spirited conversation about Anger and Rage Addiction, a number or whom having embarked on their own "Self-Pact" experiments and adventures. Heartfelt thanks go out to Emily, Hannah, Hardy, Joely, Stewart, Mike, Patrick (recently passed), Doc, Suzanne, Julie, Lew, Jill, Helen, Don, Steve, Zack, both Johns, Marshall, Tom, Charlie, Anne, Bill, Jeanne. Also, my gratitude is abiding for all those who participated in course offerings of this material at the Alcohol and Drug Summit in Bismarck, North Dakota in September 2012, and at the New England School for Addiction & Prevention Studies in Willimantic, Connecticut in June 2013. The author takes delight in being in the presence of such engaged, intrepid companions along the road to self-discovery.

Contents

Foreword xi

Prefatory Statement on Anger and Rage Addiction. xv

Anger and Rage Addiction & the Self-Pact 1

Afterword: The Irrepressible Human Psyche 103

Foreword

My dear readers and (possibly)
my fellow anger and rage addicts,

It is a privilege to share with you ripening perspectives on Anger and Rage Addiction, and a treatment approach, arising from these perspectives, called the Self-Pact which, given four years' experience thus far, appears to offer some hope of remediation for, and healing from, this hapless condition.

In sharing with you this outlook and approach I draw on both personal experience–mine and others'–and professional perspectives that I have sought out to explore. On the personal side I simply state that I have been subject to this affliction and paid out a lot of suffering in wrestling with it over many decades. As my own experiences (and consequences) gathered their unremittingly painful returns, alongside them a certain, gradual honing of awareness continued to sharpen and deepen, leading, cumulatively, to a new, more comprehensive recognition of what I was dealing with. Over time, my personal perspectives have also been deepened in manifold ways by the shared experiences of others in professional and personal settings.

The aggregation of professional perspectives has been a part of my quest for greater understanding, assuming (as I did at the outset) a rather naïve hope that definitive answers to the problem of anger and rage would be arrived at. While theory and insights ever abound, treatment that actually works in situations like mine (and so many others) was not to be found. This led me, initially, to experiment on—and with—myself, the guinea pig for testing out a sudden flash of insight that came to me amidst a sense of my own hopelessness when all other areas of remediation had been found wanting. In the four years since, this insight has taken on a name: The Self-Pact—and has been broadened into its own approach to the problem of Anger and Rage *Addiction*. This approach has provided substantial amelioration of destructive behavior(s) in my life and in the lives of others who have tried it.

So . . . at the four-year point, I share this with you, adding the voice of personal experience (unabashedly—if somewhat nervously—choosing not to hide behind a Ph.D. and professional standing), drawing also on other voices of those who have tried the Self-Pact, all of which, and all of whom, are forming, collectively, a new "voice choir" with a message of empirically grounded hope. Along the way, the "personal' and the "professional' cross paths and entwine from time to time, but the most important ingredient is the authentic voice of real experience, discovery and adventure, ever minting itself anew—new concepts and actual access to a true, healing possibility through grounded encounters in the real world—both external and internal—for this pervasive problem of human suffering.

May this little missive, and the monograph to follow, contribute something useful to you in the personal sphere, the professional sphere, and perhaps both together—in service of goodness always.

Yours, with the love of a kindred spirit,
Stephen Rich Merriman

Pioneer Valley, Western Massachusetts
May 31st, 2013

Prefatory Statement on Anger and Rage Addiction

Anger and Rage Addiction can be conceptualized as operating along a range of manifestation. At one end of this range is "chronic anger," manifesting as a steady-state hostility of constant corrosiveness and toxicity. At the other end of this range is "acute rage," manifesting as an episodic triggering phenomenon, leading to spectacularly explosive, inappropriate and destructive acts. Most manifestations of Anger and Rage Addiction consist of amalgams of both components. The same energy of addiction underlies both.

ANGER AND RAGE ADDICTION & THE SELF-PACT
New Lights on an Old Nemesis

The out-workings of anger and rage addiction are corrosive and toxic, cumulative and cyclical. They are characterized by the phenomenon of "triggering" (a neurological process that is faster than rational thought and conscious vigilance can track), conscious motive (which makes the surfacing of anger and rage seem plausibly rational and justifiable), efficacy (transitory: the immediate consequence of a triggered episode often appearing to achieve, at least briefly, conscious intention), consequences (in which the pushback—either active or passive—of affected parties gives rise to shame, guilt and remorse: the implosion of self-esteem), fervid attempts to undo the damage (all of which are part and parcel of *reloading* in preparation for the next triggered unleashing), and then the eruption of the next triggering episode ... and on and on it goes.

────────────────

None of this is new behavior. Anger and rage are stitched into the fabric of every human being on earth, arising first as a neurological discharge in the life of an infant—a response to acute or unmet needs of early life, along with a shedding by the body of excessive, "stacked" energy and sensory stimulation—and building on these origins throughout toddler-hood and early childhood. In abusive households, rage and tantrums may even be a first attempt—primitive though it is—to establish a self-other boundary: to erect, and enforce, a "No Trespass!" zone regarding abuses and torments, and those who inflict them.

In later childhood, adolescence and on into adulthood, self-righteous indignation and lust for vindictive triumph are often a part of conscious mindset in and around the phenomenon of triggering, inseparable from the need to experience oneself as possessing, and asserting, personhood amidst the perceived absence of outer-world respect and validation. Curiously, there are often, in hindsight, varying degrees of amnesia in the picture if someone who has unleashed is asked, subsequently, to recall events or provocations leading up to the moment of triggering, along with the events immediately following.

In the world of psychology, anger and rage that reach levels of manifestation considered pathological are categorized as "disorders" (impulse disorders, etc.). The range of "treatments" the professionals have brought to the table from the world of mainstream psychology, as served up by mental health practitioners, have largely been aimed at awareness-building combined with behavioral modification stratagems in which "triggering" is the enemy, and all efforts are to be exerted to keep triggering from happening.[1] As well intended as such approaches may be, they have, on balance, fallen short due to an underestimation of the dynamics of what they are attempting to influence—the basic neurological reality of triggering itself (to be set forth presently).

From "Disorder" to "Addiction":
The First New Light on an Old Nemesis

As early as the late 1950s alcoholics and drug addicts who had found their way into recovery via two "mutual help," Twelve Step-oriented fellowships, Alcoholics Anonymous and Narcotics Anonymous, had begun to take note, in their recoveries, of addiction dynamics that were playing out in non-alcohol and non-substance-based areas of their lives. These dynamics had an eerie, familiar resonance to them—notwithstanding their being operative in behaviors to which the moniker "addiction" had not previously been applied.

Sufficient numbers of recovering (in terms of alcoholism and drug addiction) individuals made this connection between what their active alcoholism and drug

---

1) A summary by the American Psychological Association (APA) of what may be considered current state-of-the-art/best practices for dealing with anger and rage can be found online at: http://www.apa.org/topics/anger/control.aspx.

Note that all these various suggestions are rationally based, anger and rage mitigation strategies.

addiction had been like, and what was besetting then in various behavioral, though non-chemically-based areas in their "sobriety," that the first Twelve Step fellowships concerned primarily with behavioral addictions started to come into being. These included Gamblers Anonymous (addressing compulsive wagering [and the many forms this can take]–founded in 1957 in Los Angeles, California), Overeaters Anonymous (addressing compulsive overeating–arguably a "hybrid" addiction involving both behaviors and substances–founded also in Los Angeles in 1960), and Debtors Anonymous (addressing compulsive indebtedness–which formerly emerged in 1976, in New York City).

That same year (1976) Sex and Love Addicts Anonymous (addressing areas of addictive sexual behavior and "love" addiction–i.e., morbid dependency) started in the Greater Boston (Massachusetts) area, and other fellowships aimed at the "sex addiction" area that started around this time include Sexaholics Anonymous, Sexual Compulsives Anonymous and Sex Addicts Anonymous.

Unlike the areas of alcoholism and drug addiction, in which grassroots self-help initiatives (Alcoholics Anonymous and Narcotics Anonymous, respectively) helped pave the way for the emergence of the professionalized field of alcoholism and substance abuse/drug addiction treatment, the professional community was largely blind to what the grassroots movements in behavioral addictions were empirically pointing to—the need for the addictions treatment field to expand its sense of vision as to what an "addictions treatment field" really needed to consider and address, as a part of its professional calling or mission. In fact, for several decades following the inception of these behaviorally-aimed self-help initiatives, the "addictions treatment field" considered itself to be dealing solely with alcoholism and chemically dependency, a remarkable under-reaching given what, at the grassroots level was staring it in the face. Continued on page 8

A little aside

Another significant development, from the quasi-professional side, transpired in the fall of 1977. In *Psychology Today* (a journal that follows, and reports on, trends in popular psychology), an article was published the subject of which was physical exercise: specifically, running. This article mentioned (for the first time I know of) the endorphin release—the "runner's high" that accompanies extended running (and, by inference, accompanies all intensive, extended exercise)—noting, with concern, that some runners who had exercised to the point of injuring themselves had (a) forced themselves, against medical advice, to continue to run, regardless of their existing injury, (b) experienced symptoms of withdrawal (especially depression) if they could not run, and (as it turned out), (c) these runners were chasing the endorphin high at the risk of compounding their physical injuries.

It is also interesting to note that, also from the psychology direction, there were a couple of thoroughly New Age/experimental therapies that had their day in the sun during the 1970s and 80s. They both (for lack of a better descriptoid) would fall under the overall heading of "expressive therapies." The first of these was the proliferation of weekend-long "feelings regression workshops," which ran a range from (on the milder end) confrontive "T-groups" (therapeutic encounter groups), to (on the heavier end) yogic breath-work-oriented groups that engendered regressive episodes in which emotion, of whatever stripe, could be "released." While not expressly a therapy for anger and rage disorders (let alone "addiction"—of which their was no conception in that era regarding 'behavioral addictions') the sense, and intent, was one of "detonating" the release of emotion. I recall, in the late 1970s, exploring one such offering in Northern Vermont. I described a persistent, unaccountable "issue" with anger and rage, and the would-be group facilitator chimed in, prematurely and declaratively, "So you want to detonate the bomb." I was caught off guard by his remark. Despite a relative lack of insight in those days, I responded, "Like, how about defusing it, instead? Believe me, I'm very good at detonating it; there's no victory in that outcome for me." I did proceed to do the workshop, and wound up, while lying on my back on a mattress on the floor, screaming my ass off for eighteen hours or so. It certainly was "expressive."

The other therapy of note from that era, though also not expressly directed towards anger and rage issues, was Arthur Janov's "Primal Therapy"—again, very expressive. His book *The Primal Scream* (1970 was subtitled: *The Cure For Neuro-*

sis. (Janov was no shy violet.) The theory was that if one could get in touch with, and unleash, "primal" pain and suffering, there could be a once-and-for-all release of this pent up energy, and one would emerge "neurosis free!" I knew a few people (more than a few, really) who threw themselves into Janovian groups for the purpose of accessing primal pain, and releasing it with great physicality. The odd thing, though, was that the discharge of primal energy (if that's what it was) led to a refractory period—certainly pleasant enough—but this state was not an end state. There was subsequent "build-up" requiring further immersions into primal-screaming. Those who became repetitive at this exercise either convinced themselves (or, more likely, were told) that they hadn't yet gotten to their "core pain," and hence had yet to reach the holy grail of once-and-for-all release and freedom (maybe next time, huh?), or, more likely, they were (unbeknownst to them) coming up against one of the structural givens of the human psyche: that energy continues to "stack-up" no matter how successfully one has purged a prior buildup. (Even the Dalai Lama, enshrined as one of the more placid, poised, collected presences on our planet, revealed in a recent interview that he occasionally loses his temper—and, that he would not trust anybody who denies losing his or her temper. [http://abc-news.go.com/GMA/video/dalai-lama-angry-13400561]). The best of the Janovian groups held to the admonition, "Feel the feelings, but don't act on them" (*in the outer world—* my emendation). In hindsight, there is something about this admonition that suggests that Janov, and those who adopted his techniques and philosophy, were on to something, but the ramifications of what it is to "feel" the "feelings," and why not act (out) on them in the outer world, begged significant clarifications, which were not forthcoming at the time.

So what was it that those who were in recovery from alcoholism/drug addiction via Alcoholics Anonymous (AA, started in 1935 in Akron, Ohio) and Narcotics Anonymous (NA, started in1953 in—once again—Los Angeles) noticed about certain of their behaviors that carried such eerie hallmarks of their earlier behavior as active alcoholics and drug addicts? And ... might there be some "take away" from these awarenesses that would inform a more salutary understanding of anger and rage? In other words, could traveling the conceptual path from the behavioral signatures of anger and rage "disorder" to anger and rage "addiction" yield anything useful?

Here's what these early, recovering grass-roots pioneers noticed:

1) They noticed that they were engaging in certain behaviors to enhance pleasure (as do we all), reduce pain (as do we all), remain functional and/or to ward-off symptoms, either physical, psychological, or both, of withdrawal or deprivation.

2) They noticed that they were requiring, over time, increasing levels of absorption into indulgence activities to achieve the desired effects of indulging. In other words, they noticed that they were building

tolerance to what they were craving, which required greater intensity of active engagement to breach.

3) They realized that they were experiencing loss of control over the rate, frequency and duration of their behavioral indulgences:

Rate = how much "xyz behavior" they were doing during any given episode.

Frequency = how often indulgence episodes would occur.

Duration = how long (temporally) an indulgence episode would last.

4) They noticed that when they were separated or cut off from their "source of supply"—the means and the opportunities to indulge and act out—they would experience symptoms, either physical, psychological, or both, of withdrawal that could erupt in any dimension of human experience: mind, body, spirit and heart.

5) They recognized that levels of life unmanageability—a negative quality they thought they had left far behind them when they had gotten clean and sober in terms of alcohol and drugs, were back—unbidden, unsought, not knowingly cultivated or desired. Negative consequences of an increasingly troublesome nature had returned.

These five criteria for recognizing the existence of behavioral addictions were derived entirely from the realms of alcoholism, drug addiction and chemical dependency. These criteria weren't the only ones to cross the divide from substance-based addict to non-substance-based addict, but they were the major ones, and sufficient for making an exacting diagnosis of any behavioral addiction.

There was another "takeaway" from the applicability of these criteria—one not even fully recognized at the time by those who were pioneering the establishing of behaviorally focused Twelve-Step fellowships in the 1950s, '60s and '70s. Here it is:

Once one "crosses the divide" via discovering that the signposts of addiction (the five criteria) can exist in the purely behavioral realm, rather than exclusively in the alcoholism/drug addiction and substance-abuse-involved behavioral realm, the recognition naturally follows that *"Addiction," as a phenomenon, can no longer be described reductively in terms of "having an addiction to" "this substance" or "that behavior." Rather, as a concept transcending* both *substance and non-substance behaviors, Addiction, unavoidably, can only be cast as an outworking of a certain kind of ENERGY!!* The channels through which this ENERGY!! is expressed may be either substance-based or non-substance based (or both), but the common denominator is neither the substance or chemical compound, on the one hand, nor necessarily any specific behavior, on the other. The common denominator is the ENERGY!! itself. Addiction, in other words, is primarily reducible to the presence of an ENERGY!![2]

This ENERGY!! has many qualities that, in the aggregate, comprise it, and hence, there are a number of ways to view, or consider it. Perhaps drawing most immediately on the circumstances that give rise to the recognition of behavioral addictions in the first place (arising, as we know, from the grounded experiences of those in recovery from alcoholism and drug addiction), the quality of the ENERGY!! which most immediately stands out is that of

---

2) It is true that Addiction can also be usefully reduced to a study of the interactions of neurotransmitters in the brain, and, more generally, throughout the entire body. Much contemporary brain imaging research has noted identical patterns of neuro-cranial transmission that are activated when either substance- or non-substance-based behaviors are involved. Both the "Addiction Energy"–"ENERGY!!"–viewpoint, and the biochemical/neurotransmitter viewpoint are complementary approaches to clearer understanding as to what is at work. The "Addiction Energy" approach, however, may be more immediately in tune/synch with the subjective realities an addiction-prone person is confronted with, and is easier to grasp, while the neurotransmitter model must be somewhat abstractly conceptualized, and, therefore, stands at more of a remove in terms of being of practical application regarding influencing addictive behaviors via non-pharmacology-oriented treatment (always to be preferred in the treatment of addictions).

displaceability. The ENERGY!! is utterly displaceable. It can shift around from one channel of issuance to another, setting up its theater of operations (for acting out) either blatantly, or with exquisite subtlety. Borrowing from the old terminology (and origins) of early 20th Century psychoanalysis, this thoroughly recognized characteristic of psychical energy is called "displacement."

Those who were in recovery from substance-based addictions often reported that obsession and compulsion to use their prior compounds-of-choice (alcohol or anything else) had been removed. The sense of reprieve, and remission, that accompanied the removal of obsession and compulsion could, if it continued long enough, come to feel like "cure" regarding their prior substance-based acting out.

What they hadn't realized, however, is that while obsession and compulsion in their former areas of active addiction may have been "removed," *ADDICTION ENERGY in its raw, elemental form, had not been*. In other words, only one channel, or outlet, through which Addiction Energy had found expression was "removed," *but not the underlying ENERGY!! itself.*

To put the matter another way: Within the acting out of any addiction there is often the subjective report of feeling possessed by the need to indulge (in whatever form of addiction is bedeviling one). The need/drive/

compulsion/desire/hunger/craving/obsession to act out can be experienced as an alien force that has taken on a life of its own, regardless of conscious intention, espoused morals and ethical principles, assimilated education, religious training and cultural conditioning, along with any belief systems that would contribute to a conscious intention to *NOT* indulge and act out.

With the alleviation of obsession and compulsion in any specific area of addiction, there would be a sense of release from the subjective experience of being in the grips of the possession—the very drive to act out itself. One might conclude that the energy—or symptoms—that were experienced as having taken on a life of their own during the active phase of a particular addiction, were gone.

But were they? With the recognition that addiction dynamics (in the forms of the five criteria) could show up in the non-chemical addiction realm, and the following recognition that (therefore) addiction is, in its fundamentals, an ENERGY!! rather than a specific "addiction to 'this', or 'that,'" came the further, unavoidable awareness that Addiction Energy itself—The ENERGY!!—once launched in all its displaceable potential, has, generically, beyond any particular manifestation or outworking of it (and any specific apparent, healing experience in offsetting it) a life of its own, working to its own ends regardless of human intention.

So this little foray into addiction theory, as informed by the increasingly recognized existence of behavioral addictions, has something crucial to offer regarding Anger and Rage Addiction. Here it is:

The ENERGY!! that underlies Anger and Rage Addiction is autonomous. It has taken on a life of its own and this independent existence works to its own ends, regardless of the conscious intention of the body's presumed occupant—the "anger and rage addict."

The ramifications for "treatment" of Anger and Rage Addiction given the autonomy of Addiction Energy—the ENERGY!!—underlying it, are profound.

First, most, and possibly all, current treatment approaches to anger and rage "disorders" (the term applied from the DSMs—and reflexively accepted by mental health treatment community) are centered on rationally based, behavioral modification and behavioral management strategies designed to prevent triggering—the instantaneous unleashing of an anger and rage binge—from happening. While some behavioral modification approaches may, in passing, term anger and rage disorders as "addictions," they let the matter go at that—as if just using the word "addiction" somehow is clinically descriptive—as if there is a some automatic, shared, general understanding that "addiction" simply designates a behavior that is compulsive. This is, to put it mildly, sloppy, unthinking usage of a profoundly useful, descriptive, diagnostic, and even prescriptive, term. The larger essence of what "addiction" really means: the five diagnostic criteria constituting the outworking of an autonomous, unleashing ENERGY!!—goes wholly unrecognized.

Without this crucial understanding, the aim of treatment then becomes keeping triggering from happening. All efforts, usually focused on intellectual understanding, are to be directed at helping an anger and rage disordered person developing *rationally* based, strategic interventions—mechanical rules, "thought-stopping" techniques, intellectual insight into issues apparently fueling rage and anger, becoming aware of early cues, signs and signposts that one is building up to triggering, mnemonic tools, analytically based understandings regarding behavior, etc.—all are to be employed to keep triggering at bay, and away. While these stratagems, tools, techniques and insights can, for some afflicted people, render triggering a less frequent occurrence, in the aggregate they are insufficient to the task at hand; indeed, even the task, or goal, is an incorrect one, for "rational understanding," of the intellect, cannot take the place of acquiring *experiential knowing*.

The sad fact is that if the ENERGY!! is autonomous—has taken on a life of its own—the goal of mitigation based on rational use of the intellect, however well intended, is not attainable. ADDICTION ENERGY—"ENERGY!!"—WILL OUT! The big question is: If triggering is inevitable regardless of one's best, sustained efforts to eliminate, suppress or otherwise squelch it, how does one relate to this ENERGY!! when—not if—triggering occurs? The starting point on the playing field has changed. It no longer starts with "How not to trigger?" It starts with "When—whenever—I trigger, then what??"

Because the anger and rage addict is, unbeknownst to him or her, at the mercy of Addiction Energy—the ENERGY!!—which, *unto itself*, unleashes as it will, the difficult, experience-derived recognition is, "I can not keep myself from triggering."

Let's put this in a context. A person with this form of addiction is driven by Addiction Energy—ENERGY!!—but doesn't know it. Rage binges are typically laced with what appears to be plausibly sourced resentment (as spurred by encounters with the "slings and arrows of outrageous fortune"), lust for vindictive triumph (a holy crusade to slay any perceived wrongdoing and smite the forces of the infidel), and self-righteousness (an extraordinary basis for seizing ephemeral moments of self-fulfilling grandiosity). If we go to the five criteria that are diagnostic for Addiction, we see that anger and rage binges can *appear to serve* a number of plausibly legitimate causes, or "issues." For instance, explosive triggering can create, momentarily, quiet or peace (as those around us are shocked into silence), impose (via volume and intimidation) a sense of order, provide (pathetic and illusory though it is) a sense of "manhood" (or "womanhood"), assert control over one's immediate, perceived tormentors and environment, be a prelude to creating (or, more likely, extorting) "intimacy" (arising from contrition-based discussions with spouse or lover), establish dominance (a sense of momentary mastery over a person or situation), and so on. While these "issues" all have the trappings of a certain legitimacy to them in terms of what could, let's say, be individually worked on within the province of psychotherapy or counseling (after all, who doesn't need to find experiences of "peace and quiet," or find an inner security about "being a man" or "being a woman," be able to stand up to, constructively counter or offset those situations in which we are bullied or disrespected, experience intimacy with another who really knows us, loves us and accepts us such as we are, and develop some mastery in dealing with other people and situations, day in and day out)—all of these plausible sounding, legitimate-appearing "issues" are, from the standpoint of an actively acting-out anger and rage addict, a deception—just red herrings, diverting attention away from what the underlying reality is. The underlying reality is, once again, this: ADDICTION ENERGY–ENERGY!!–WILL OUT! It will readily assume the trappings of "legitimate issues" to make its surfacing and outworkings take on an air of legitimacy. "Issues," however, and their relationship to unleashing, become suspect and, once Addiction Energy–the ENERGY!!–has taken on a life of its own, irrelevant. Such "issues" may exist, but *the outworking is Addiction Energy—ENERGY!!, pure and simple—and carries on as an independent variable from "issues."*

Once Addiction Energy–the ENERGY!!–has taken on a life of its own, its sense of urgency comes to rule, requiring "more" of the indulgence to achieve the desired effect. A perusal of an anger and rage addict's history of triggering/unleashing will commonly invoke the presence of a series of negative consequences arising from prior outworkings of anger and rage, in response to which attempts to "right" things or "set things straight" become more and more perseverative, and triggering thresholds become lower and lower. Anger and rage become, increasingly, "one-size-fits-all" reactions to *any* situation of discomfort, however imminent, minimal or subliminal, and to *any* "issue" (either real or imagined). The ramping up of frequency in unleashings is ever more pronounced, with the payoff from each unleashing becoming more and more desperately clutched and ephemeral. "More and more" works "less and less." This is a direct analogue, in the behavioral addictions realm, to the development of tolerance in substance-based addictions.

Other features that characterize Addiction Energy—the ENERGY!!—as it surfaces in the form of Anger and Rage Addiction include *amnesia, loss of control* (over rate, frequency and duration of triggering episodes), *the "negative rush" phenomenon, and increasingly negative consequences* occurring over time, *a/k/a* life unmanageability, also referred to as *"progression."*

Amnesia

It is more than curious to note, in those with Anger and Rage Addiction, that when a person "comes to" following a triggering/unleashing episode, there is often little concrete recollection of what the thought process was which ostensibly led up to the triggering episode. Following an episode, it is not unusual for an anger and rage addict to be largely amnesic as to precipitating causes and conditions. A closer questioning may lead to responses that are clearly patch-work confabulations as to provocations, sequence of events, and so on.

Not unlike the use of alcohol or chemical compounds to alter mood (and hence one's experience of reality), this prevalence of significant amnesia as to "what led up to ...?", "what happened ...?", etc. suggests that "triggering" is a near instantaneous activation of body chemistry and neurological pathways that are not terribly consonant with everyday consciousness. Anger and rage experiences are built around this neurology, and encoded within it. "Its" knowledge and comprehension of episodic misadventures is not readily shareable with the body's more matter-of-fact neurological constellation. They are different worlds indeed!

The amnesia following anger and rage triggering/binges/tirades, in the midst of which the person may have been—in addition to being very highly destructive—highly rational, highly articulate, highly "tuned in" to personal history (at least as this pertains to previous anger and rage binges in which he or she has participated—which are a part of his or her personal history), and completely oriented and attuned to his or her current milieu, are as analogues to "black-out" phenomenology as it occurs in active alcoholism and drug addiction. Utterly different, discrete neurologies can arrange that body in decidedly pluralistic, though largely separate, ways.

From the standpoint of "withdrawing" from an anger and rage binge and trying to recall leading-up-to-triggering and episode details, the anger and rage addict's attempts to recollect (re-collect) details are not unlike someone awakening from a powerful dream trying to re-call the dream's details. An immediate sense of tangible-ness as to the dream's contents (perhaps leading to a con-clusion that "there's no need to write up the dream now; the details are so crisp that I can get to it later without los-ing any of it") quickly gives way to recollection becoming ever more fleeting as what seemed "tangible" slips over the edge into unconsciousness, beyond retrieval.

This amnesia and the stark, discretely separate ar-rangements of the body's neurology to which "trigger-ing" gives rise (triggering being simultaneously a prod-uct of, and a cause of, this very neurology—that's how quick and immediate it is), may be rightly considered dis-sociative phenomenology for which corollaries abound in a wide range of human behaviors.

Loss of control

This seems obvious. A person who rages is not in control, either of shaping the expression of emotional energy, or shaping the expression of personal behavior. *This outworking* of what, in a child, would be termed a temper tantrum *is brought on by the triggering phenom-enology that launches in less than one-seventh the time it takes for rational faculties to be deployed to head it off.* In other words, an anger and rage addict is at the mercy of his triggering neurology. It picks his fights for him, and reason must "catch up" with it if any rational, "current moment" context is to be applied to it. When triggering detonates, the limbic system's surge bypasses the frontal cortex—momentarily short-circuiting the seat of rational, conscious thinking. *It takes seventy milliseconds (70ms— 1/14th of a second) to trigger, and by the time "reason" knows that this "is happening"... it's already happened. It's old news. Triggering already occurred four hundred-thirty milliseconds (430ms—nearly half a second) earlier.[3] Hence the futility of attempting to head off triggering via approaches geared to "rational understanding," willful control, and "informed management." Good luck; it ain't gonna happen.*

An appreciation of the neurological impossibility of heading off triggering via rational means leads to several acknowledgments. The first is that, as mentioned previously, Anger and Rage Addiction exists in a way that leaves the person who has it at the mercy of their triggering neurology. Such a person does not consciously choose the stimuli that trigger (which can be multi-variant and almost always unconscious)—let alone the "issues" about which s/he feels is why s/he is unleashing.

---

3) Neurological/synaptic network response data source for this monograph:

http://plato.stanford.edu/entries/consciousness-temporal/empirical-findings.html

His or her triggering neurology determines them instead. S/he has no rational say in the matter.

Existing at the mercy of one's triggering neurology is a perilous proposition. It's no longer (nor probably ever was) a matter of "if I trigger," but, rather, *"when* I trigger." In fact, for the anger and rage addict "triggering" is the most predictable—and expected—aspect of the whole syndrome. It is the essence of most all of the outer-world unmanageability that follows suit on unleashing episodes—domestic violence, divorce and split-ups, traumatized children (and adults), loss of jobs—and sometimes of careers—crimes of passion, civil or criminal (or both) consequences that inevitably follow suit. An anger and rage addict is never the master of his own dominion. His neurology is—and his neurology doesn't necessarily have his best interests at heart—"don't know from nuthin'" about "best interests."

It's not that there are no attributable, plausible-sounding causes for these eruptions. As previously mentioned, there are many. Here, once again, is a representative (though hardly complete) list, some entries of which have already received passing mention: lust for vindictive triumph; getting drunk on self-righteousness; rage for order; rage for power; rage for control; rage for intimacy; rage for manhood (or womanhood); rage for peace; rage for quiet; rage for dominance; rage to intimidate (bully); rage to punish (beat up on); rage at injustice; rage at obstruction (frustrations in all their forms); rage at people (including other drivers, family members, employers, co-workers); rage at (perceived) authority; rage at stupidity, idiocy, ignorance and asshol-ery (in all its forms); rage at places; rage at things; rage at situations; rage at circumstances; rage at institutions (the government, the church, school etc.); rage at ideas (philosophies, systems of belief, etc.); rage at abusers and perpetrators (of any description); rage at betrayal (breach of trust); rage at abandonment; rage at lack of being appreciated, acknowledged or recognized; rage at being criticized;[4] rage for rage; rage for destructiveness; rage for bloodlust, rage for self-hatred. The palate of "justifiable causes" is rich, indeed! How remarkable that anger and rage unleashing can be such a "Johnny-One-Note," one-size-fits-all response to such a varied bag of provocations! And yet, the very fact that the "response," *regardless* of the varied nature of claimed issues and prov-ocations, is *always* the same, is strongly evidential that the underlying ENERGY!! exists unto itself, regardless of claimed "causes" in the outer world. Indeed, we're re-

---

4) Regarding the preceding "rage at's" on this list, it's rage "at" rather than rage "against." As a reactive, triggered phenomenon, compulsive anger and rage is almost always reactively "at" something rather than purposefully "against" something. Their manifestations give evidence of an underlying, pervasive sense of impotence—a pro-found lack of power and self-efficacy in the anger and rage addict.

ally not talking, here, of "responses" (which have a deliberative quality to them) at all. Rather, we're talking "reactions"—immediate reactive discharges. As plausible as such "causes" may seem as "underlying issues," rational recognition of them in the throes of triggering are always ex-post facto, because, as previously set forth, the rational foundation for this level of comprehension involves frontal cortex processes that are *slower* to engage than the triggering neurology itself. Once again, "Triggering" is independent of rational causation, and is unstoppable. *The real essence of loss of control in terms of Anger and Rage Addiction finds its provenance in the neurology of triggering. For the anger and rage addict the absence of control over triggering is the hard-wired reality. And ... there is nothing an anger and rage addict can do about it.*

But wait! There's more! In addition to such tidy, plausible "explanations" as are listed above, there is a whole other *modus operandi* that is the actual reality at work in most—maybe all—anger and rage addicts. And here it is:

The Negative Rush

While such attributes, motives and causes for anger and rage triggering as "lust for vindictive triumph," "getting drunk on one's own self-righteousness" (i.e., slaying the infidel), "rage for order," "rage for power," "rage for control," "rage for intimacy," "rage for manhood (or womanhood)," "rage for peace," "rage for quiet," "rage for dominance," "rage to intimidate (bully)," "rage to punish (beat up on)," "rage at (perceived) injustice," "rage at (perceived) authority," "rage against idiocy/stupidity/assholery" (in all its forms), "rage at obstruction/frustration (in all its forms)," "rage at people," "rage at places," "rage at things," "rage at situations," "rage at circumstances," "rage at institutions," "rage at ideas" (and philosophies), "rage at abandonment," "rage at betrayal," "rage at frustrations" of all sorts, "rage at being unappreciated or unrecognized," "rage at being criticized," and all the rest, provide at least the appearance of plausibility, and legitimacy, for the unleashing of anger and rage, there is a whole other category of attributes that eschews all the aforementioned, and gets to the heart of what triggered anger and rage is really, at its fundaments, all about. *The subsuming category is "Rage for Rage."* Categories that are subsumed by it (which include a number of the aforementioned) are "Rage for Destructiveness," "Rage for Self-Hatred," and "Rage for Bloodlust."

What is unique, and revealing, about the "Negative Rush," and the bold-faced categories that fall under this heading ("Rage for Rage," "Rage for Destructiveness," "Rage for Self-Hatred," and "Rage for Bloodlust") is that episodes of wanton destructiveness as delivered by unleashings under each of these headings delivers a "high"—a "rush." "Highs" are usually designated by a "+", *but this kind of "high" is really a negative (-) high—a sickening downer that delivers a stomach-churning, adrenalin-laced fierceness which "gets off" on the very destructiveness of what(ever) mayhem it is creating in the outer world. In other words, the "Negative Rush" "gets off" on "rage for the sake of rage," "destructiveness for the sake of destructiveness," "self-hatred for the sake of self-hatred," "'laying-waste to' for the sake of 'laying waste to,'" "blood-lust for the sake of blood-lust."* [5]

While all the other plausible sounding explanations for anger and rage unleashing—"lust for vindictive triumph," "getting drunk on one's own self-righteousness" (slaying the infidel), "rage for order," "rage for control," "rage for power," "rage for manhood," "rage for womanhood," "rage for intimacy," "rage for peace," "rage for quiet," "rage to dominate," "rage to intimidate (bully)," "rage against injustice," and on and on—may, as previously stated, don the mantle of, or carry a cachet of, a certain legitimacy from the standpoint of psychological assessment, representing at some level "issues"—grist

---

5) "Rage for blood-lust" is experienced as the fury of homicidal intent, and sometimes climax, and "self-hatred for the sake of self-hatred" is often experienced as an affirmation of the deepest truth one has been taught about oneself in childhood—that one is worthy only of being hated.

for the mill of psychotherapy–ultimately, in an anger and rage addict, they also are subsumed by, and fall under the category of, the Negative Rush. The distinction here, however, is that *these legitimate-sounding categories lead away from recognition and acknowledgement of the "destruction-for-destruction's-sake" reality that underlies all of them. This distinction is one way of highlighting the difference between anger and rage "disorders," and Anger and Rage* Addiction, *in which destructiveness—just like the ENERGY!! underlying it—has taken on a life of its own, and "gets-off" on itself.*

It is not as if remorse and guilt are inauthentic experiences for anger and rage addicts as an aftermath of emotional, mental, physical and spiritual carnage. *Yet such rending emotions and the self-loathing, wholesale contrition and penitence that may follow upon them are merely parts of a larger cycle—that of reloading for the next triggered outrage.*[6] Neurology determines that the destructiveness "will out," regardless of resolutions that it not. Repeat-

---

6) I wish to credit *Vicious Circles Manual: Anger Management for Men* (Stephen C. Simmer, Ph.D., 1999) for helping sensitize me as to the role shame and anxiety play as apogees in the cyclical process of triggering, unleashing, and reloading. Simmer focuses on this process with specific reference to anger and rage as their outworkings seek to procure love, order, respect, peace and freedom. Simmer's work has enriched my understanding of the cyclical nature of these events, and is likely the best of those approaches that fall under the "applied rational understanding" category.

ed episodes amplify and reinforce the Negative Rush, and deepening experiences of self-reviling only further heighten the sickening in-rush of negative affirmation that comes from repeated destruction. Destructiveness, from the standpoint of the anger and rage addict, unto itself, is a sickening, potent drug.

Few, if any, are the anger and rage addicts who have any idea of how truly condemned they are. An autonomous ENERGY!! unleashed via Triggering Neurology, outstripping in its efficiency less efficient rational attempts to subdue it; Amnesia, leading to a murky, hazy, polluted, diverted sense of causality and awareness as to what truly underlies triggerings, the Negative Rush, with its sickening relish of destructiveness for its own sake, contributing ever greater "highs" of reinforcement to the "lows" of destructive acts—such a juggernaut is a "devil's playground" of evil outworkings and their grotesque, sickening, toxic consequences.

Hopelessness of the condition (progression)

Thus far we've covered a lot of ground, tracing, after a fashion, the empirical justification for the broader term "Behavioral Addiction" to its roots in the drug addiction/alcoholism recovery/self-help movements in the 1950s, '60s and '70s—grounded in the experiences of those in recovery from substance-based addictions who had the courage–and the necessity–to recognize what was befalling them in behavioral areas as "addictions," notwithstanding the tone-deaf response of the professional addictions treatment community (not to mention the mental health community generally) at that time. Then, based on the presence of addiction diagnosis–meeting the five criteria for addictions as derived from alcoholism and drug addiction–we transitioned into a recognition that "Addiction," at its fundaments, is an ENERGY!!– regardless of its channels–either substance-based or purely behavioral–of issuance. We applied the term "displacement" (the old psychoanalytic term) to the quality of this remarkable ENERGY!! to shift around from one channel to another, and we made mention of the lamentable truth that the release from obsession and compulsion to act-out in any specific area of addiction–the happenstance that one may experience in this regard–does not constitute "cure." While any given manifestation of acting-out may go into remission, the ENERGY!! remains. Reprieve, if it goes on long enough, may come to feel like cure, but it never is.

This led us into the area of Anger and Rage Addiction (really a sub-category under the much more extensive, and subsuming category "Behavioral Addictions"). Focus on Anger and Rage Addiction, it was noted, stemmed from particular interest in this area (exceeding, surprisingly, thus far, the overall interest regarding other behavioral addictions, including sex addiction, "love" addiction, et al.).

With more focus on Anger and Rage Addiction, we waded in to describing some of its particularities: triggering phenomenology and amnesia, various categories of "issues" that can seem (incorrectly) to be the causative factors, when all they do is provide a veneer of legitimacy to anger and rage unleashings, and, most importantly, the Negative Rush reality, in which destructiveness takes on a life of its own, and, as self-reinforcing, becomes an end in itself. It was suggested that this characteristic, above all others, is the one that most cleanly delineates Anger and Rage *Addiction* from the imprecise, sloppily applied catch-all diagnosis anger and rage *disorder* (under the more general heading: impulse disorders) and its spurious offspring.[7]

7) For example, in DSM-IV, various components of anger and rage-related diagnoses are spread willy-nilly across a whole range of diagnostic categories, each constituting its own set of criteria. Here they are: Oppositional Defiant Disorder and Conduct Disorders, Attention-Deficit/Hyperactivity Disorder and Conduct Disorder (in children and adolescents), Psychotic Disorder, Bipolar Disorder, Antisocial, Borderline, Paranoid and Narcissistic Personality Disorders, Adjustment Disorder with Disturbance of Conduct, and Intermittent Explosive Disorder. Regarding addressing Anger and Rage Addiction and its phenomenology as a *cohesive* syndrome, what a "dog's dinner" of concatenations all this is. As someone once said, "A camel is a horse designed by a committee" (and this hardly does justice to the camel).

Finally, in consideration of this juggernaut of autonomous ENERGY!!, Triggering Neurology, Amnesia, Loss of Control, and the Negative Rush, we arrived at a recognition that the anger and rage addict lives, de facto, in a hopeless, condemned state. Compounded consequences of anger and rage unleashings leave a permanent legacy of tragic outcomes, along with ultimate demise for the anger and rage addict—but not before psychical infection has been passed along to subsequent, unsuspecting generations, who are then predisposed to perpetuate the evil.

A "wake-up" call

It is time for an obvious, though disheartening, point. In absorbing and assimilating all the previous information and observations, we have necessarily drawn on rational faculties. In exercising our own ability to comprehend— to gain a comprehension of—Anger and Rage Addiction we have deployed our intellectual resources. The problem is this: Perhaps (hopefully) some useful knowledge has been presented, including various concepts such as amnesia, the Negative Rush, the elapsed time difference between the triggering neurology (about 70 ms) and the cognitive/"rational" neurology (about 500 ms). But ... in learning about and pondering such things, our own process has been largely cerebral—and intellectual. So...

we may have learned, for instance, about "triggering neurology," but our learning has necessarily been ponderously rational, and *slow*. In other words, what we have learned may bear relevance to our condition as anger and rage addicts, BUT, none of what bedevils us—especially the triggering neurology—has been influenced in any substantive way by what we have come to know. What knowledge we have gained may "enlighten" us, but not one jot and tittle of it transfers into any improvement vis-à-vis dealing with our Anger and Rage Addiction from the standpoint of defusing it. We have, as yet, gained nothing through this intellectually-based knowledge—*unless it deepens into experience-based **knowing***.

But what does this mean? Simply this: *All the knowledge we have acquired, if it is worth anything at all, serves to highlight—not how to deal with and defang anger and rage triggering and outbursts—but, rather, the futility of any attempts to subdue them.* Knowledge, in this regard, leads *not* to self-assurance, but to a deepening sense of our own dilemma, crisis and hopelessness. If everything I have presented thus far deepens your sense of futility and despond, then perhaps *those* emotions begin to signal the shift from "rational knowledge" to "experiential knowing." That deep-in-the-gut feeling that we are cursed, and condemned—regardless of our best, most noble efforts to stem the corrosive tide—to head-off leaving a toxic legacy of heartbreak, violence (emotional and physical)—along with the continuous reaping of scorched-earth consequences: the acid-suffused outworkings of our indomitable behavior, our Anger and Rage Addiction—may be—just maybe—serving to prepare us to attempt something new—something previously unattempted, something heretofore unrecognized as being possible—as even existing as a possible avenue to try.

Let's name it: *enter the Self-Pact.*

The Self-Pact: the Second New Light on an Old Nemesis

The Self-Pact is a radical approach to the problem of Anger and Rage Addiction. It honors "triggering" as an ineluctable reality of life for the anger and rage addict. *The Self-Pact can be implemented by any anger and rage addict, acting on his or her own, drawing solely on personal, inner resources.* The Self-Pact can also form the basis for informal (perhaps "mutual support" or self-help-oriented) groups of anger and rage addicts to arise, to come together for mutual aid and sharing of experience, strength and hope—the foundational elements of a "healing community." The Self-Pact can, as well, also be introduced to an Anger and Rage Addiction-prone client within the context of life-coaching, counseling, and individual or group psychotherapy.

The Self-Pact can only be successful if an anger and rage addict has reached a profound level of despair, hopelessness and desperation concerning both his or her personal, extended history of anger and rage episodes and their consequences, combined with prior attempts—rigorously embraced—to deal with his or her "anger and rage problem" via anger mitigation/behavioral modification approaches and strategies right alongside acquiring self-knowledge and rational understanding about "anger and rage" and their consequences. For a Self-Pact candidate, all such approaches based on rational understanding, cognitive restructurings and reframings, and strategic interventions have proven insufficient to stem the tide of such polluting effluent. A conviction of utter futility regarding *ever* being able to master, or subdue, triggering events, anger and rage unleashings and all attendant toxic consequences—regardless of one's most honest, fervent desire to not act out this way—must have soaked into the marrow. A sense of being condemned to live out an agonizing life of broken hearts, broken relationships and tragic losses and alienations—of being fatally, irremediably flawed and forever beyond redemption's reach—must have taken root in awareness, penetrating both the rational and emotional life of the anger and rage addict. All hope—as may have attended prior efforts—that triggering, outbursts and unleashings, verbal, emotional (and sometimes physical) violence can be controlled or reined in, have been dashed. The conviction arises that there is nothing left to try—that one is (colloquially speaking) terminally "fucked," cursed, damned, with nowhere else to go and nothing left to try. All this, collectively, is the *sine qua non* for the anger and rage addict who stands any real chance of being helped by the Self-Pact.

In other words, a person has to have been repeatedly chewed-up, mangled and mauled by his or her Anger and Rage Addiction and its toxic outworkings over an extended period of time for the Self-Pact to hold any possibility of working.

What is the Self-Pact?

So ... what is the Self-Pact?

The Self-Pact is a deal one makes with oneself—between "me," and "me."

It consists of Four Declarations.

The *First Declaration* starts with the recognition, admission, acceptance and declaration to oneself that:

1) *"I am a person who triggers, and there is nothing I can do to keep triggering from happening."*

NOTE: This means that "triggering" is accepted as an unavoidable reality in the life of an anger and rage addict. For better or worse (richer or poorer, 'til death do "us" part), it's "baked in the cake"—an immovable reality which can not be begged, borrowed, cajoled or otherwise persuaded to "take a hike," or "leave well enough alone." It's just "there"—a given.

The *Second Declaration* of the Self-Pact moves into the Pact commitments proper:

2) *"I make a pact with me that whenever (not 'if') I trigger I will acknowledge and accept the energy of triggering as being present in me. I agree to accept the presence of this energy."*

NOTE: This component of the Self-Pact is an agreement between "me" and "me" to acknowledge and accept the presence of triggering/anger and rage energy—ENERGY!!—as a predictable, and therefore expected, presence. The full presence of this energy is acknowledged and, after a fashion, welcomed.

The *Third Declaration* of the Self-Pact is:

3) *"When (not 'if') triggered, I/we agree that I/we will go to any lengths to spare the outer world:*

> a) the creation of any (further) victims, and
> b) any further victimization of past victims of my/our anger and rage."

NOTE: The pact to go to any lengths to not create any further victims and not add any additional victimization to past victims with "my" anger and rage is a sacred commitment. This aspect of the Self-Pact is NOT an attempt to in any way squelch or suppress the energy– ENERGY!!–of anger and rage itself. This energy is fully present, and welcomed to be so. In "sparing the world the creation of any additional victims," and foregoing "any further victimization of past victims" of our anger and rage, *the energy—ENERGY!!—is held, in full potency, while others are spared.* This is true regardless of any perceived (either actual or imagined) provocations from the outer world that may be claimed as having created or led to the triggering event.

The *Fourth Declaration* of the Self-Pact is:

4) *"In full acknowledgement and acceptance of the Third Declaration (above), I/we agree, when triggered, to "ride the energy"—ENERGY!!—of anger and rage: to let this ENERGY!! show me what it wants me to know, whatever kinds of experiences it wants me to have with it, whatever emotions and feelings it wants me to en-*

counter, along with any awareness it wants to arise in me—by opening myself to let this ENERGY!! drive itself, along with my full awareness and participation, INWARDS.

NOTE: With the resolution, as a component of the Self-Pact, to "spare the outer world the creation of any additional victims" and foregoing "any further victimization of past victims," even while acknowledging and accepting the presence of anger and rage energy–ENERGY!!–that energy now has only one direction where it can move–and that is INWARDS. "Riding the energy" is letting it, and "us," be harnessed to one another on an inward, mutual excursion.

These Four Declarations:

1) I am a person who triggers.
2) Whenever I trigger I will acknowledge and accept that the energy–ENERGY!!–of triggering is present in me; I agree to accept the presence of this energy.
3) When triggered I/we agree that I/we will go to any lengths to spare the outer world the creation of any new victims of my/our anger and rage, and spare the world any further victimization of past victims.
4) When triggered, I/we commit to "riding the energy"–ENERGY!!–of anger and rage. I/we agree to let the energy of anger and rage–the ENERGY!!–

show me what it wants me to know, take me wherever it wants to take me on the inside, including whatever kinds of experiences, feelings, emotions, and awarenesses it wants me to have, by opening myself to let it drive itself, along with my full awareness and presence, INWARDS.

Collectively, these Four Declarations, between "me" and "me," *are* the Self-Pact.

The "sacredness" of the Self-Pact, and some additional perspectives

The Self-Pact is personal, sacred, and held as such. Establishing it "between 'me' and 'me'" is a sacred act. If an anger and rage addict is desperate enough (as previously noted) the sacredness of such a commitment becomes a *felt* experience—no maudlin sentiment here—just a centered focus of attention combined with utter determination, taking on, in the aggregate, an unmistakable, integrated emotional hue. But regardless of whatever emotions may be swirling around the Self-Pact as it is inaugurated and entered into, the Self-Pact usually constitutes the last chance for an anger and rage addict to salvage something redemptive—something of value—from having lived out such a profoundly destructive course. It had better be a sacred commitment; the next stop beyond, should the Self-Pact fail, is the final bequeathing of a toxic legacy, the poisoning of unsuspecting, subsequent generations, and self-annihilation in the bottomless pit of redoubled self-hatred and tragedy.

A note about "me" and "me" ("you" and "you")

The Self-Pact, birthed as we know in desperation—I won't get tired of repeating this—is a pact between "you" and "yourself"—"you" and "you." In phrasing the participants in this way, the Self-Pact acknowledges a reality of the human condition: *Insofar as our neurology is constantly rearranging in accordance with our experience of our "moods" (each "mood," having, within us, its own discrete neurological constellation), we, each one of us, are, at some level, a pluralistic entity.* The "rageful I" has a very different level of neurological (along with endocrinal/hormonal) engagement than the subsequent contrite, guilt-ridden, remorseful "me." The body our moods express through may be singular, but there are very many neurological/glandular/hormonal presences that make themselves felt within each, and every, human body.

So, in addressing and forging a Self-Pact between "me" and "me," the Self-Pact is a trans-ego—or at least an intrapersonal, or trans-mood—agreement. It is knowingly entered into not solely by "me"—the presiding (as far as I know) ego-presence of the moment—but by those components of my being (which does, indeed, include "me" and my neurological constellation), *along with them and their respective neurologies that are operative in, collectively, our anger and rage-infused realities.*

In other words, the Self-Pact is established between "me," and all concerned inner arrangements—neurological and hormonal—of "me."

Admissibility and inadmissibility

As a passing thought, it is at least possible that some of the destructiveness of the energy of anger and rage addiction may owe itself to the very fact of this energy's—ENERGY!!'s—inadmissibility as something to be "listened to" and "taken seriously." If there is any interior logic operative within the triggerings and unleashings of anger and rage, it may be at least in part attributable to the forced attitude inhabiting customary ego consciousness as it tries to abide by the cultural stereotype of "unacceptability" regarding the expression of this ENERGY!!, leading to wholesale attempts to shunt or thwart any outworking of it—to cut it off at the roots—rather than being more openly accepting of the energy's existence and even willing to be "taught" by it regarding "our" story and history. The consciousness inherent in addiction energy—ENERGY!!—would, presumably, experience a cumulative frustration and exasperation at being repeatedly stymied, shunted and suppressed out of expression, knowing that this constriction is really an attempt to shut it out of existence—to abandon or exorcise it. "Amp-ed up" fury would be a consequence of such repeated attempts to "be gotten rid of... ." Of course, one assumes a certain presumption in "taking the part" of Addiction Energy and rendering it a voice. But it is possible that an inner dynamic of this sort does exist within anger and rage energy—the ENERGY!!—itself.

What the Self-Pact gives rise to re: triggering

If we detach, for a moment, from assuming the voice of anger and rage ENERGY!! itself, let's consider what the Self-Pact gives rise to in the heat of a triggering episode. The Self-Pact has now been set in place, has been made 'holy' by a ceremony of some sort—either an occasion set aside and privately solitary, or (maybe) an occasion shared with an understanding friend, or perhaps a therapist. (Regardless of whether any one else is there to witness such a ceremony, the Self-Pact is still made solely—soul-y—between "me" and "me." No promises or commitments are being made to second or third parties. Nor is the presence of any one else's being in attendance a necessary precondition for the Self-Pact to be set in place.)

So ... we're playing on a different playing field now. Triggering is to be expected, and accepted (because, regardless, it can't be stopped). If one tries to "track" the current of triggering, it is possible to stay consciously attuned to a build-up of some sort (tension, anxiety, lower-case anger, etc.). However, since the neurology of triggering supersedes—takes precedence over—rational processing power (a slower process than triggering), the best consciousness can do around tracking triggering goes something like this: "I'm feeling uncomfortable, tension arising with me, anxious, on edge—anger starting to rise—I've triggered, I'm already triggered." This is to say that because the acute moment of triggering bypasses, outflanks—is far too quick for—the inner powerless rational faculty to track it, a person leaps from a rational vigilance of feeling anger "building"—and knowing it—to "coming to" *to having already triggered*. In other words, the actual moment of triggering is amnesic, and consciousness/awareness can only catch up to it (having arrived [back] on the scene after the fact of triggering).

To return to the first sentence in the preceding paragraph—the one which begins with "So ...," the Self-Pact, through having been previously set in place, is what is amalgamed with consciousness when consciousness "catches up with" the reality that triggering has occurred.

Oh ... but the Self-Pact doesn't start with: "I'm triggered; I guess I fucked up." Not at all. The Self-Pact instantly resonates inwardly with "I'm triggered. OK. I feel your presence. Where do you want to go? How do you want to dance? Creating victims in the outer world is 'out,' but I'm here to ride you inwards if that is where you want to go—to take me. Let's dance."

And what does it mean to "dance" with anger and rage energy—ENERGY!!—unleashed by triggering? That, my dear reader, is an individual adventure, and not one to be described for you in the manner of some blueprint of specifications you should, or are meant to, follow. It would be presumptuous of me to take it upon myself to tell you anything in the manner of "what has to happen" when the Self-Pact has been made operative, and is there *to knowingly work with* the energy of anger and rage—ENERGY!!—rather than try to snuff it out or keep a lid on it. I can't, in good conscience, "go there."

But I can offer some possible contours of what the Self-Pact has brought to others—of what kinds of experiences are *apt* to happen—and I am willing to do so. This does not take anything away from the sacredness and individual nature of what awaits you, of your own journeys and discoveries that may unfold for you via the Self-Pact. Rather than present the Self-Pact experience as a narrow, one-size-fits-all path, generic observations and reports may better serve to present it as a very broad highway of individual experience(s), discoveries, insights, awarenesses, and (yes) adventures.

So here we go.

"Rational knowledge" vs. "experiential 'knowing'"

Many people, when faced with encountering an unknown, will try to establish a basis for rational understanding and comprehension about what they may be embarking on or confronting (or being confronted by)— even, reflexively, attempting to compress, or transfer, anything that might occur or take shape into the "rational frame." Forging a rational concept—conceptualizing— what may be afoot can be permission-giving regarding a person's daring to venture forth, especially if the concepts are strong and take on an aura of tangible realness. *This "permission-serving" purpose may be helpful, but the habitual, reflexive attempt to reduce, via conceptualizing, life encounters to a rational level of experience constitutes the distinction to be made between "rational knowledge" and "experiential knowing."*

In terms of the Self-Pact and what it seems to foster, it is all about the "experiential" rather than the purely rational, or "intellectual."

Whenever the Self-Pact has been established (between "me" and "me"), and triggering occurs, the EN-

ERGY!! is not directed into the outer world to create victims (a condition of the Self-Pact). As soon as consciousness catches up to the reality of having already triggered (in which one's first inner statement is usually "I have triggered"), the ENERGY!!, in all its raw fury is held—not squashed. With no option to raise havoc and create mayhem in the outer world, the one direction open to the ENERGY!! is to go *inwards*.

In knowingly being available and willing to ride the energy—ENERGY!!—of anger and rage inwards, in some curious way the cooperating component of anger and rage energy to do so is forthcoming. Many variations on the theme of "inner journeys" await, and are in store—most of them unknown or unanticipated at the outset.

As we ride the current of anger and rage ENERGY!! inwards, the palette of what is available for the ENERGY!! to draw on and leaven up is remarkable.

It is hard to render this panoply of experiences into verbal language. In the immediate moment of "riding the ENERGY!! inwards" there may be crystal clear cognitive awareness of earlier episodes and milieux in which past "triggerings" have taken place.

Previous triggerings that especially pre-date one's more recent past (including relationships)—sometimes a seemingly random sample of episodes that extend very far back in one's personal history—are common.

These may unfold either as a kind of cognitively-based history-on-a-timeline, a sequence of "facts." Or ... past events may become clear as a result of the similarity of the overall *resonance*–including thought process, emotional tone, etc., in which the Energy!! of current, triggered experience–the Energy!! current, so to speak–now ridden inwards, is, in the aggregate, an experience that is somehow concentrically overlaid, in near precise alignment, on experiences that carry a similar valence at levels of psyche, affect and soma.

In contradistinction to having past history reassemble as a procession of factual occurrences along a timeline, the amalgam/concentric overlay modality actually re-creates the essential mind/emotion/body experience itself, revealing, through this resonance, the inalienable relationship/correspondence that exists between the current triggering and the whole overlay of previous ones.

The means through which these linkages are revealed–either as "factual recollection" or concentric, entire, multi-axis re-experiencing(s)–is not made by the ego consciousness–now triggered consciousness– of the person who is triggered. It seems that the energy of anger and rage–the ENERGY!!–when harnessed by conscious intention for the purpose of taking the inward journey (again, the only direction, via the Self-Pact, now open to it), in some sense is, itself, the architect of what, and how, revelations are to be accomplished. It is anger's and rage's collective trip "inwards," and "we" are its passengers.

Again, I refrain from saying anything definitive about the particularities of these inward-driven journeys because there is a high level of variation to individual experience—including idiosyncratic individual expression—in them. To be more specific would be unfair to those reading this because it might leave them trying to "measure up" to some seemingly externally imposed standard, or benchmark, rather than be drawn to making their own personal, private discoveries the journeys hold for them.

So, once again, my comments about what Self-Pact journeys reveal, or are like, must necessarily remain general and generic, with the unavoidable opaqueness that must be a part of any such presentation. Yet whatever gaps are left open are yours to fill in—the entirety of whatever is there waiting to be known, increasingly revealed to you by your own process of discovery.

Immediate benefits of the Self-Pact

One obvious point is that in honoring your agreement with you not to create victims in the outer would, nor re-victimize past victims, when you trigger—and *are* triggered—enacting this major component of the Self-

Pact has immediate benefits. The biggest of these early returns is the cessation of outer-directed violence—verbal emotional, physical (spiritual?, sexual?). The energy of destructiveness and unleashing—the ENERGY!!—is "all there," and held, but the ENERGY!! is being harnessed for the inner/inwards adventure, not acted-out on externally.

Those who are near and dear to us, and who have been our continual victims, are apt to be caught almost in a state of disbelief that the fusillades and the tirades they are so accustomed to being on the receiving end of are NOT HAPPENING.

This is in stark contrast to how it has been for others in our lives—both those who were once with us, finally couldn't take it any more, and are with us no longer, and those who are with us currently (assuming there's still anyone left).

Walking on eggshells has come naturally to these folks. They've been all too well trained by us. For those of us who tried to "control" our anger and rage triggerings by any of the anger and rage mitigation techniques along with self-knowledge, we may well, when we had been marginally successful at heading-off unleashings for (usually short) periods of time, have misled those who truly matter to us—our "good behavior" being enough to stir in them a nascent hope that a different day was dawning.

Of course, whatever hope and glow of a new dawn would be present was, always sooner rather than later, utterly dashed by subsequent triggering and unleashing—all the more so when such triggerings that "broke the truce" seemed to roar up out of nowhere, with no obvious substantive provocation—and instead, sallied forth often on the heels of an utterly intimate, close experience, as in a dinner out, intense lovemaking, or even a blissful vacation.

If we use the expression "dynamite the creek" as a stand-in for triggering and unleashing, it is easy to see that even if triggering and unleashing are, through mitigation techniques, made less frequent, the "all-bets-are-off" destructiveness of the onslaughts *when they resume* still leads to toxic outcomes that are as severe as when anger and rage binges are more frequent. On the one hand, if the "creek" is being dynamited six times a month rather than twelve time a month (a day?, a week?, a year?—the principle is the same), this might seem like meaningful progress. On the other hand, lamentably, is this inescapable fact: Each time the creek is dynamited all the fish are killed. Each "detonation" still kills all the inhabitants!

In fact, such outcomes from less frequent anger and rage triggering are even *more* injurious and toxic, because, in the more benign-appearing interim, those nearest to us are likely to have been lulled into some kind of hope that a change has occurred which will persist—hence they have let their guard down. This leaves them even more vulnerable, and more extremely affected—emotionally slaughtered—when, with their defenses lowered, they are once again assaulted. Small cause for celebration.

*But now, with the Self-Pact in place, and activated, ces-*sation, *when triggered, of violence (in any form) can lead to what has always been needed—the opportunity to expand into* cumulative *effects, the fruits of which are no longer being slain, or otherwise sabotaged, along the way.*

So ... the effects of the Self-Pact on our own immediate environment are salutary and profound. Gradually, as the Self-Pact becomes a reality that is as felt, and as actively activated as the triggerings themselves (which, of course, are ongoing), trust, in terms of emotional safety and no longer being in harms way, starts to come into the picture. All of this is a wonderful fringe benefit of the Self-Pact—all the more so because, in the past, while the desire to spare damaging others was always deeply felt (especially during the "guilt, remorse, contrition and resolution" phase of reloading) these motivations had never been sufficient—no matter how keenly felt—to stem the destructive onslaughts. *Now, with the Self-Pact in effect, they have ceased.* Triggerings are ongoing, but unleashings on the outer world have stopped. The "virtuous cycle," thus launched, in our immediate environment, is palpable.

Unfolding developments of the Self-Pact—
pathways of inner voyaging

As perhaps is becoming clear, the energy of anger and rage—the ENERGY!!—now available to carry us inwards, has work to do. An inner adventure, primarily, on many levels, experiential, leading to dimensions of awareness and comprehension—of experiential *knowing*—are now open to us to access.

The overall heading under which all such experiences— inner journeys—are subsumed could be described (if one is so inclined) as getting in touch with, or coming in contact with, "original causes and conditions." In other words, via various channels that become activated through anger and rage energy's driving inwards, realities are re-encountered in ways that are highly experiential. Such encounters place us in contact—in correspondence— with the cascading resonance of Addiction Energy—the ENERGY!!—from its preconscious origins on through developmental episodes of infancy, toddlerhood, early childhood, pre-teen, teenager, young adult, adult, midlife, and (in some of us for whom the Self-Pact is inaugurated much later in life), advanced middle-age and early elderhood.

Wow.

What channels can anger and rage energy–the EN-ERGY!!–traveling inwards, have at its disposal to reach us with its "message?"

There are many. Bear in mind that every Self-Pact journey is, at least in part, a "resonant" experience. Think of a tuning fork's being struck alongside a tuning fork of the same pitch that has not been directly struck. Sound waves from the struck–intoned–tuning fork will travel outwards from it, and the effect of "resonance"– the sound waves encountering the second tuning fork– will induce an audible–and quite possibly visible–vibration (equal in pitch, and near equal in volume) in the non-mechanically struck tuning fork. The dynamic of "resonance"–the second tuning fork being of the same pitch as the mechanically struck first tuning fork–induces the movement in the second tuning fork.

"Emotional resonance" acts the same way. Anger and rage energy–ENERGY!!–in the form of its *emotional charge* will, when inner directed, send its waves forth into "interior space." Whatever past situations, encounters or events are encoded in memory–those including other people, places, things, situations, circumstances, conditions, institutions, ambitions, ideas, beliefs, disappointments and losses, etc., which carry any emotional hue (resonance) similar to the emotional valence of the anger and rage energy–the ENERGY!!–now detonated and propagating on the inner plane, will be restimulated–will start to "vibrate" with an emotional "tenor" and "resonance" and, sometimes, "recollection."

There are two ways in which we can speak of this process. The first (as earlier suggested) can be expressed as "channels" through which the "wavelength," or resonance of the ENERGY!! is both transmitted and, if kindred resonance is there to be activated (as is almost always the case) through which the responding/corresponding resonance can make itself known. These channels include each and all of the sensory faculties–visual, auditory, olfactory, taste, kinesthetic, proprioceptive, physical sensations/touch, and intuition. Anger and rage energy–ENERGY!!–may find a corresponding resonance in any one (or more) of these areas that link either to some particular, specific preceding occurrence, or to some more general gestalt or pervasive milieu (perhaps in the manner of a watercolor wash forming the background and surrounds of a more detailed painting)–taking more the form of an environment with its overall, attendant resonance being activated.

In the case of environmental or milieu resonance, what is stirred is not one particular/specific event per se, but more the sense of an ambience that was chronic, and which constituted a backdrop for much of what transpired over some life epochs, or mini-epochs, of the anger and rage addict's personal history.

"Resonance," in any such example, may find its counterpoint in one specific sensory channel, or in an orchestration of two or more sensory channels.

With growing proficiency in Self-Pact activation when triggered (part of the "deal" one makes with oneself), such inward travels–riding the energy of anger and rage (the ENERGY!!) inwards–can unfurl rapidly.

In addition to the stimulation into activation, via resonance, of individual sensory channels of perception, there are also more delayed effects stemming from the activation of anger and rage ENERGY!! that is moving inwards.

The very fact that this ENERGY!!, far from being exorcised or otherwise peremptorily dismissed as "unacceptable" or "inadmissible," is not only expected (via triggering), but accepted into the mix of our life experience, day in and day out, suggests that, when activated, it has more time to do its work–to search for, leaven up, and put us in touch with, those other resonances that await. In other words, on the inner plane the Self-Pact permits this ENERGY!! to be loosed, into the psyche, where it propagates to do what it needs to do–without being under constraints to be "done" in more time-limited episodic fashion.

Hence, there are ambient, residual effects of this EN-ERGY!!'s being "loosed" within. The first of these (the order of mention of these effects is arbitrary) is our dream life. The Self-Pact seems to have an awakening effect on dreaming and, within dreams there exists innumerable resonances that can stir and make their existence known. But this awakening to dreams and resonances within dreams is not arbitrary. It is meaningful, for dreams are capable of conveying multi-dimensional linkages that relate, energetically, to what has become a chronic problem of self-bedevilment—our Anger and Rage Addiction. There are whole mindscapes and dreamscapes awaiting manifestation, in service of helping us gain a greater, deeper comprehension of "original causes and conditions."

In addition to our dream-life, there is an awakening of "hunches" and "intuitions" that can come to us during our wakeful hours. These awarenesses, inner promptings and inner knowings, though fueled by inwardly traveling anger and rage energy—ENERGY!!—*are not in themselves triggering*. They are, rather, enriching. One can have surprisingly peaceful feelings and emotions—not stemming from whatever immediate awakenings one is having regarding any specific recollection of a past event or milieu (as would typically attach from consciously riding the ENERGY!! of anger and rage inwards during a triggered episode)—but, rather, from the capacity, *now being made manifest, of an ability to encounter, observe, acknowledge and accept such resonances, and the awarenesses that flow from them, in a non-triggered fashion.* There is almost a pleasure to be had in discovering that this experience, as fueled by anger and rage energy itself—the ENERGY!!—is happening.

A further development as to the nature of anger- and rage-fueled inner journeys

Another challenge in attempting to describe something about the quality(ies) of these anger and rage EN-ERGY!!-fueled inner journeys involves experiences that can arise which are multi-channel or multi-dimensional in nature.

In describing the nature of the previous modality of experiencing this inner-driven ENERGY!! of an-ger and rage, the emphasis was one of discovering what sensory linkages would be stirred, via resonance, into awareness—would intrude into the current triggered experience—giving rise to the establishing of new, and *conscious*, connection between the current triggering experience and its experiential antecedents. However, there is another experiential reality that can arise (should it choose to reveal itself this way) from "riding the energy of anger and rage—the ENERGY!!—inwards."

For some of us it goes something like this: As the nodal points of resonance are touched off by the inwardly directed ripples of anger and rage energy, *these detonated, or roused, points of past anger and rage experience start to emanate their own sympathetic waves* outwards *from themselves; the current(s) of these emanating waves propagate from their source or locus within, traveling outwards.* In other words, while the anger and rage ENERGY!! of a current, triggered event travels, via the Self-Pact agreement, *inwards* from a current triggered reality in the outer world, the nodal points of past experience that are resonant with, and touched off by, the inwards-directed ENERGY!! start to travel *outwards*, in the direction of the current, "present" milieu in which the triggering took place.

So inner-directed anger and rage energy—the ENERGY!!—coursing from "the present" to "past history," finds correspondence with the energies of the past, stored in nodal points which are enlivened or awakened, via resonance, by the inward-rushing current, and these "energies of the past" issue forth their own current(s), radiating outwards, from "past experience" into "the present."

This is what differentiates Self-Pact experiences from being describable, in clinical terms, simply as "regression." In a regression a triggering event, unbeknownst and unobserved by ego consciousness, ambushes and hijacks a person into a state of immersion with an experience of the past—often the deep past. The tethers of ego-consciousness are riven through this ambush, and the person "loses touch" with the present. There is no anchorage in place to hold a person in the "here and now."

With the Self-Pact, however, a completely different order of experience unfolds. First, the absolute inviolability of the Self-Pact tenet to, first and foremost, "create no victims—no new victimizations—in the outer world," once in place, creates a firm, non-negotiable anchorage in the present—the "here and now"—the central, unfolding, current milieu.

A consequence of this Self-Pact tenet is that a foothold of ego consciousness remains attuned to the present even as it knowingly rides the energy of anger and rage (the ENERGY!!) inwards. So, one foot of awareness, so to speak, is firmly implanted in "the present," and stays here.

The inward-riding ego consciousness is immediately affected by the inner nodal points of resonance touched-off by the inrushing ENERGY!! of the current triggering episode. This activated energy, emanating from whatever the stimulated nodal points are that resonance has awakened, is now, as mentioned, moving "outwards," and it has a date with—a rendezvous to make with—that portion of rage consciousness that is, with vigilance, attending to the Self-Pact constraint to "do no outer-directed harm."

So... inner-directed ego consciousness is riding the wave of anger and rage energy—ENERGY!!—inwards, and nodal point "past" energies, set loose by the waves of inner directed energy, are radiating from their inner loci, outwards, into the present, here-and-now attentiveness of ego-consciousness. I am endeavoring to describe (as unavoidably clumsy as language, lamentably, must be) the makings of a "rush of consciousness," in which the overall triggering experience, as consciously entertained and engaged with via the Self-Pact, culminates in the *felt, experienced, recognition/realization* that THE WHOLE TRIGGERING EPISODE, INCLUDING ALL EMOTIONAL CURRENTS WHICH SURROUND IT, *IS* THE EXPERIENCE OF CHILDHOOD. This experience is **TOTAL**. It knows no distinction between past and present, between new anger and rage and old, between infant-toddler-child-adolescent-adult-elder—between present and past. The time dimension is completely collapsed, and *the reality of the underlying, now fully surfaced lineaments of character are starkly revealed through their being simultaneously experienced*. This is anything *but* simple regression. This is not insight-based, objective knowledge. *This is direct, experiential, participatory knowing*. This "knowing" has two sides, simultaneously occurring: One finds oneself thoroughly immersed in a ubiquitous reality, and: *Thoroughly immersed in a ubiquitous reality, one finds oneself.*

Self-Pact realizations: what do they lead to?

What do Self-Pact realizations and knowings lead to? A larger question that naturally stems from these inner experiential journeys and encounters has to do with the extent to which—if at all—the very phenomenon of triggering itself is somehow altered. This question will be more fully addressed presently, but I'll venture a few brief comments here.

To be sure, there are positive feedback loops that develop. One, previously given specific mention, is the milieu that comes to be established keying on the fact that "I am safe to be around." Triggering, while never easy for other people to be in the presence of, no longer carries with it the threat or risk of being emotionally and mentally mauled, or physically intimidated and abused. This is a tremendous acquisition, and a development that is independent of whatever inner Self-Pact adventures we are encountering and experiencing. This part of the Self-Pact, in which the outer world is spared a new—or restimulated—roster of victims, puts an end to emotional rupture, broken hearts, betrayal of trust(s) and personal safety, environmental chaos and violence, broken dreams, broken relationships, obvious grounds for divorce and split-ups, along with all manner of anger- and rage-fueled self-sabotage behaviors at home, at the office (including during the commute back and forth) and anywhere else we go in the outer world. Not a bad roster of profound interpersonal and external world impacts stemming from " ... sparing the world ..." And none of this even considers the changes that may be taking shape on the inner plane.

Inwardly, there is the adventure of personal discovery attaching to "riding the ENERGY!!" of anger and rage inwards.

These, as we know, take the basic forms of sensory channel experiences and awarenesses, and whole-gestalt experiences. I'll speak to sensory channel experiences first.

One of the great delusions of triggering with anger and rage unleashings is that the supposed causes and goals for these lashings-out are held as being in the external world, and anger and rage, it logically follows, are realized, sudden attempts to redress, rearrange—and maybe destroy—the "external landscape." This leads to momentary impact and possible satisfaction of the "reasons" for exploding—followed by push-back, kick-in-the-teeth consequences.

However, with the Self-Pact in place, every triggering is instantly acknowledged and seized upon as an opportunity to ride the energy of anger and rage–the ENERGY!!–*inwards*.

The simple fact is this: Each (and every) time this inwardly-ridden ENERGY!! leads to some resonance-based connection with a nodal point within–whether this be a felt connection with even some meager aspect of sensory experience (sight, sound, smell, touch, taste, intuition, sensation, perhaps something else entirely), the awareness that this has happened, and that this new domain has been a direct result of the Self-Pact–riding the ENERGY!! inwards–*each time this happens* is *a different resolution to a triggering episode than has been heretofore experienced.* This truth–including both what(ever) is encountered and what it is that has made the encounter possible–what has enabled it to happen–is not lost on the experiencer. Destructive outer-world workings of anger and rage ENERGY!!, now redirected to the inner plane, have led to a very different outcome, and conclusion, for this one triggering episode. This is a big discovery. One has lived one's way into knowing that the awareness that has been won by this process–even in the simplest incidence of it–has great worth to it. It has been won by a discipline that honors the ENERGY!! and what it is capable of revealing, rather than mindlessly wreaking havoc with it, or otherwise condemning, stuffing or trying to exorcise it.

For those of you who are "visualizers," a simple, little color analogy suggests itself: "Red" is usually taken to be the color of blind rage. "Red Rage" is volatile, destructive, roiling. The triggered unleashing of rage into, and on to, the external world, is always "Red Rage." But ... when the triggered ENERGY!! of rage is held in full potency, and ridden inwards, "Red Rage" transforms into "White Rage," *which is hotter, more intense, and more focused*, than "Red Rage"—and "White Rage" has the power to reveal, and then cauterize, open wounds, and, in the fullness of time, heal them.

So ... the discovery that inner-traveling ENERGY!! can lead to memory-based awarenesses—that this is possible to even the smallest degree—casts anger and rage energy (ENERGY!!) in a whole different light. Outer-world mayhem gradually is giving way to inward adventures of discovery—*with the ENERGY!! of anger and rage being the guide, not the culprit*.

A further observation to be cited regarding riding the ENERGY!! of anger and rage inwards—being led via a triggering event and resonance-awakened nodal connections into some new sensory perception (and the possible awareness and insight that may attach to this)— is that, once a new linkage between this inner traveling

ENERGY!! and an "awakened" nodal point becomes a *conscious* awareness, the stridency of what, at triggering time, was completely attributed to external factors, is now seen/experienced as having its roots, a priori, in a far deeper—and older—level of experience, primitive consciousness and developmental memory. When this connection is forged, the stridency of whatever external factors have been held as having been the precipitating cause of the triggering lowers its volume—often quite markedly.

In other words, there is something about getting in touch/being in touch, in even slight ways, with an inner experience which hews close(r) to "original causes and conditions" that has an ameliorating effect on the ENERGY!! itself, along with whatever current, external factors have been taken to be precipitating causes of the triggering episode.

Sometimes, what may start as "meager encounters" comes to reveal major sections of the "mainspring" driving what was set in motion before any sort of linear thought process, and comprehension, had arisen in the life of an anger and rage addict. Obviously this "mainspring" involved the experiential milieu—the rage, frustrations, tantrums, extreme desires, unmet needs and demands, and possibly any (and all) abuse and neglect—of infancy, toddlerhood, and early childhood, resulting in multifarious, and numerous, stimuli each of which, either individually or in combination could, unto themselves, become triggering stimuli.

For instance, any given anger and rage addict's history of deep-past trauma, unmet needs, abuses and neglect would be felt–experienced–not so much as specific traumatic events and indignities (though episodes of such events would sometimes find their way into conscious memory), but as *components* of such events–meaning (for example) smells; tone, timbre, cadence and volume of voice(s); particular noises; room ambience, including paint color or wallpaper patterns on walls; rug patterns, lighting; time of year; kind of weather; holiday or kind of event being observed; sometimes a sense of eager expectations and enthusiasms dashed; scent, texture or color (and location) of certain foods; sense of being an onlooker to someone else's being abused or in danger; whatever music was in the air; whatever video was audible and visible; and on and on.

In Self-Pact immersive experiences that opened a portal into such an early, pre-thought, "pre-self" realm, came the recognition–the experiential knowing–that *the set number of potential triggering stimuli stemming from any traumatic occurrence in the life of an infant, toddler or young child was impossible to arrive at, for* each *component of such an experience—every dimension and particularity of it—could, in itself, constitute a "trigger."* The deep past held so many resonances which, in the unsuspecting anger and rage addict, could be detonated by potentially any event or circumstance suddenly encountered in the "present."

With this recognition came an appreciation of the fact that even if, somehow, one could learn to master "being triggered" by vigilance directed at any well recognized source of pre-triggering buildup (in itself a daunting unlikelihood)—that even if this were possible, such a mastery of one pathway of "triggering sequence" would be insufficient to stem the toxic tide, for too many triggering stimuli, encoded in the numerous dimensions and particularities of experiences of ancient past trauma and rage/tantrum episodes, lurked beneath conscious awareness, ever at-the-ready to detonate into the present amidst any current experience that might resonate with one (or more) of these encoded dimensions and particularities of the past.

Perhaps this reality goes further in shedding some light on why, thus far with the Self-Pact, though unleashings on the outer world have, for all intents and purposes, ceased, the frequency of in-the-moment-launched triggering has not.

Regarding the ongoing frequency of such triggerings, in the larger scheme of what may be possible, it may simply be too soon—too early in the experiences of those who have made the Self-Pact and are using it (nearly four years as of this writing)—to tell if this characteristic of frequent triggering is the final outcome. One might, as yet, hope for something better.

Despite the state of current discovery re: Self-Pact outcomes, we can, however, report, at the very least, that the ENERGY!! of anger and rage, harnessed in this way—and permitted to assume a didactic function—*is* capable of filling this teaching—and revelatory—role, and each new connection to a resonant nodal point "on the inside," however ephemeral or more extended the inner journey attending to any given triggering episode may be, is a fulfillment of a portion of this potential. The experienced fact that the ENERGY!! can connect to something "on the inside" that runs deeper, and is more salient, than the previous conviction that provocations from the outer world provide the "complete explanation" for an anger and rage episode, appears to serve, at least for a time, to "satisfy" anger and rage ENERGY!!'s *own need*. This, obviously, is a far different outcome for an anger and rage episode than external world mayhem.

These "outcomes"—again, despite what has been thus far described (and however early it may be in the development and utilization of the Self-Pact to speak convincingly or worthily of long(er)-term outcomes of total immersion experiences)—are very hard to describe, because they involve an immersive totality that, at times, is akin to being "struck dumb" by their multidimensional intensity, and the complete in-the-moment gestalt which they *are*.

More on the "total immersion" experience

The total immersion experience, if encounters with it thus far by a small number of people who have braved Self-Pact initiation contain any grounded truth, is that they tend to arise after the Self-Pact has been in utilization for some significant period of time—at least weeks, perhaps months, and (more likely) over the course of several years.

Hence, the earlier, invoked "inward" travels of anger-and-rage-ENERGY!!-journeying almost always involve nodal point detonation via the resonance of inwardly traveling "triggered" ENERGY!!, and the sensory experience that nodal point detonation brings to consciousness as liberated nodal point energy moves "outwards," leading to sensory-based awarenesses which constitute increasing levels of "experiential knowing."

In terms of what is known (at the level of present knowledge) about the process of Self-Pact journeying, one does not graduate from partial sensory enhanced awakened experience into the other reality of total immersion experiences. Indeed, as far as is known the partial sensory-based awakenings continue to occur with no apparent reduction in frequency. They may always be more numerous than "total immersion" ones.

But ... somewhere along the line, the total immersion experiences start to arise. It does not seem necessary, nor advisable, to in any way try to force them into happening. They may be just a natural development of the shifting neurology–cumulative concomitants of Self-Pact evolution.

Perhaps a level is reached where, quite suddenly, what have been unitary sensory channel awakenings and developments proceed to suddenly assemble and orchestrate all of a piece. When this happens the consciousness of the anger and rage addict suddenly transcends a focus on individual memory channel developments, and grasps, as an entirety, the complete experience that is more fully reverberating in resonance.

As mentioned previously in this monograph, triggering, when this happens, increasingly leads to a near immediate recollection that *the experience of triggering itself, and all the sensory components enlisted via resonance,* are *the experience of childhood.* They are crystal clear as the template of subsequent character formation, preceding the overlays of personality characteristics that subsequently came into being–characteristics which often, unto themselves, were adaptations—often unconscious—to the presence of the ENERGY!! of anger and rage, or simply unrelated to it altogether.

It may seem "obvious" to make an experiential connection between, say, the "triggering" in an adult body and the tantruming of an infant, toddler or young child, but drawing simply this parallel—this level of restimulation—understates the immensity and surge of what the "total immersion" experience signifies to the person who has it. This is not merely a revisiting of childhood tantruming (though total immersion experiences do carry, in part, this resonance). It is an experiential return—or, rather, *a coming forward into the present of the ENERGY!! of "original causes and conditions."* Hence, the totality of such an experience is not limited to "tantrums." It includes them, but, perhaps even more presciently, it includes the whole milieu around them—ambience, context, monolithically present emotion—all factors present not just within a tantrum, but within the whole childhood itself.

Putting all this—attempting to—into verbal/written language just about makes me ill, for in endeavoring to do so I am all too keenly aware of language's insufficiency in capturing the fierceness and intensity of what is, at heart, *experience*. So much of this experience is lost in the (any!) attempted translation into the symbolic language of "words"—a far remove from the vitality and immediacy of wordless encounter. But, in the current circumstance of writing a book about the Anger and Rage Addiction and the Self-Pact, this medium is all that is available to me.

So I continue. The percentage of triggerings, and subsequent inwardly ridden ENERGY!! of anger and rage that lead to total immersion experiences, seem to increase, somewhat, once this level of experience is opened (maybe as an intention of anger and rage ENERGY!! itself). Also worth noting is that these experiences start to recur closer and closer (temporally) to the actual moments of triggering—of being aware that we have triggered. One is still "present" in the environment and context in which the triggering occurs (home, office, with spouse, lover, children, friends, strangers in the outer world, etc.), but the total immersion reality and its recognitions are so powerful and perfusing and complete that there is an even *less* likelihood of violent acting out in the outer world when they "hit" because the experiences themselves and the awarenesses and "knowings" they carry and engender are just so rich, revealing and engrossing.

The nature of deeper realizations and encounters,
and experiential "knowings"

What are the deeper realizations/encounters/experiential "knowings" that come out of—indeed, ARE—these complete immersions? They vary (as might be expected) from individual to individual. The "original causes and conditions" of each anger and rage addict are unique. At the very least, however, it is safe to say that such awarenessess of in-the-moment realizations, as *felt* experience, are foundational events that form the basis of who that person is at his/her fundaments. The immersive realities are the watercolor wash backdrop—pervasive, surrounding, suffusing—of whatever the subsequent overlays of personality may be.

Such monolithic, massive experiences of oneself may, for instance, be the immersive recognition—bursting in startling realization—that "I am a person who hates," or " I am soaked through with self-hatred; I was taught to hate myself," or "I just don't like people," or "I just can't stand having to be around people." Again—translating such monolithic experiences into words unavoidably cheapens—may even appear to trivialize—what these experiences *feel* like, and *are*, as experientially encountered via the Self-Pact. And, once again, I make mention that *such experiences need never be forced.* They are evolutionary awarenesses and encounters and they arise as we are ready to stand the heat and urgency of their reality, which, simmering, and sometimes boiling, beneath the level of our everyday consciousness, is, and has always been, our own reality as well... *Not* easy to go there, be there, and come back—or (another way of looking at this) having "them" come here, be here, and then recede—but this path, via the Self-Pact, is open to us if we have become sufficiently sickened at the spectacle of what our Anger and Rage Addiction, as untreated, has already wrought—and where it, and we, wind up if nothing further can be done to stem the tide of such caustic and contaminating effluent.

Gaining increasing familiarity with the territory of interiority and the experience(s) encountered there

In both areas of "riding the ENERGY!!" of Anger and Rage Addiction inwards: the awakening of specific sensory channels via nodal point resonance, and the collective all-of-a-piece experiences in which a number of sensory dimensions suddenly correlate into a complete immersion—repeated visits to each territory, respectively, engender an increasing familiarity with each mode of experiencing. In a sense, each kind of inner journey becomes, owing to its nature, something to which the inner traveler becomes increasingly acclimated.

Once the delineations of these two types of experience become clear, it follows naturally that their scope and in-the-moment impact become *digestible*, and assimilable by ego consciousness.

Of course *it is an open question as to whether ego consciousness appropriates into itself these inner experiences, or, rather, it is ego consciousness, itself, which is appropriated and, to some extent, momentarily made one with, becoming assimilated into—and by—these experiences.* Here resides the riddle of the relationship that exists between egoic identity in everyday life, and a kind of equivalent, though off-scene, consciousness which is ever operative below the threshold of ego consciousness—*until* we ride the ENERGY!! of anger and rage inwards, there to discover, through resonance, this very consciousness itself, along with the "knowing" that we are never not in correspondence with it, for "It" is "I", and "I" am "It".

This increasing familiarity now ameliorates the sense of dread and foreboding that all anger and rage addicts who have resorted (thus far) to the Self-Pact feel at the outset, regarding the very prospect of, when triggered, holding the energy of anger and rage—the ENERGY!!— and "riding it inwards."

What about triggering—frequency, severity, duration?

And what about triggering? Has the phenomenology of triggering been affected in any way as a result of the Self-Pact? Are there effects on the frequency and stridency of triggering that develop cumulatively as a result of repeated, inner "ridings of the ENERGY!!?" The answer to this question at this point of discovery is two-fold—both "Yes," and "No."

The "Yes, something indeed has changed, is new or has been added" to the triggering mix is that triggerings, per se, are not feared so much for their destructive potential. Make no mistake; triggering continues to command profound respect as to its destructive capacity, but it is no longer so feared. Let's put it this way: The ENERGY!!, in terms of its destructive potential, still exists as a respected concern. What's "new" about this is that the energy— ENERGY!!—shows itself as being capable of engendering didactic awareness/experience-directed encounters. It can function as a bit of a psychopomp, in this regard. *Hence this energy—ENERGY!!—has revealed itself to have a functional aim of leavening consciousness rather than mindlessly working towards destructive, scorched-earth ends.*

The fact that the energy of triggering–the ENERGY!!– does not automatically result in mayhem, but can be, in-the-moment, near-instantly "ridden," lends an increasing awareness that a toxic legacy, carrying in its train a string of heartbreaks, ruptures, emotional and physical violence, toxic waste-dump poisonings along with mountains of unfixable damage, need not be the unrelenting, unavoidable, consequence of "triggering."

So "triggering," comes the discovery, can be tolerated and withstood—and harnessed to good purpose. Therefore, one can fear it less.

The "No" part of the response to the question goes in a different direction. Here it is: Triggering has not ceased, nor is it necessarily any less pressing and strident in-the-moment. Triggering is triggering, period. Something detonates inside, regardless of the presence, or absence, of external provocation or intrapsychic justification, and ... triggering continues to carry the full valence of anger and rage (as it always has). Over the four years (to this point) that a small number of people (self-diagnosed anger and rage addicts) have been living out their Self-Pact commitment (to themselves), this appears to be the case.

Nor, as mentioned, has there (as of yet) appeared to be any lessening of the frequency of triggering events, as if some kind of "mastery" over the occurrence of "triggering proper" (the goal of all rationally-based "treatment" for anger and rage "disorders") has been achieved. Not so far ... and maybe never.

Short of the hope that such a change in triggering (itself) might be realizable, there is nevertheless a bit of a silver lining still in the mix: *It is possible to co-exist with triggering—with being a "triggerer"—and to live to good purpose regardless.* One can still be at the mercy of triggering neurology and events, and, utilizing the Self-Pact, cease, when in the throes of triggering, from inflicting oneself on the outer world and contributing to the toxic waste-dump of human tragedy. The mindless outcomes that (our own history has shown us) were surely accruing in our lives during our previous, either untreated or inappropriately treated condition can be held, for the rest of our sojourn here, in abeyance.

How lovely it would be if the ENERGY!! of anger and rage addiction would somehow be exorcised, and we could all live in a state of quiescence undisturbed by "dynamiting the creek." The "bliss" of exorcism is indeed seductive, because if a condition (like Anger and Rage Addiction) were removed, we presumably could continue on in our lives without any particular vigilance or effort—at least in terms of having to deal with triggering, any longer. But this, at least at present, does not appear to be possible.

Daily renewal of the Self-Pact

For the toxic legacy of untreated Anger and Rage Addiction to be kept out of the picture it appears that sustained commitment must be maintained to the Self-Pact on a daily basis. One needs to acknowledge the Self-Pact, and renew one's commitment to it—to oneself—upon awakening, before venturing out into the outer world at any level (including going downstairs for breakfast). The Self-Pact is confirmed, made operative, and enacted anew—*daily*.[8]

---

8) Sometimes a little self-styled prayer upon awakening can instantly serve as a "sign in" for another day of Self-Pact commitment. (There's no harm in eliciting support from "the better angels of our nature"—and any other beneficent forces that may be in attendance.) One that has evolved for me is, "Dear (Loving-Power-that-be), Please help me to honor the Self-Pact today, my commitment to me. Please help me not to act-out destructively this day in the outer world, nor destroy what I have in my life that I love and cherish and is meaningful to me. I ask you for this assistance despite my very real capacity to be destructive—which may even include my conscious desire not to be." Such a prayer can be used, and adapted, as needed. Another wonderful, general-purpose prayer that can help focus conscious intention is the "Serenity Prayer," a pragmatic mainstay of the self-help community. A longer form of this prayer (one of many variations) which has proven helpful, is: "God, grant me the Serenity to accept the things I cannot change, Courage to change the things I can, and the Wisdom to know the difference. Grant me patience for the changes that take time, appreciation for all that I have, tolerance for those with different struggles, and the strength to pull myself up and try again, one day at a time."

The longer contours of Self-Pact awakenings

While it is still early in the collective experience of Self-Pact utilization to know what the longer-term contours of this commitment may be, there are at least a few discernible awakenings that may be harbingers of longer-term developments.

The first involves early indications regarding how men who are anger and rage addicts and commit to the Self-Pact come to see themselves as "men," and the second is how women who are anger and rage addicts come to see themselves as "women."

For anger and rage addicts who are male, the identity with "manhood" has often been a largely unconscious, reflexive one—or at best only semi-conscious. These men have, historically, derived, or rather, *absorbed*, their sense of manhood from cultural role/gender role stereotypes often fostered by mainstream media outlets, including journals and magazines, the cinema, music/rap and music videos, the video gaming culture, along with countless websites and blogs catering, sometimes blatantly, and always (at least) implicitly and subliminally, to what "being a man" is. *The ways and values of "what it is to be a man," as transmitted via these media, are always* **collective** *ones—*"success" (power, prestige, sex and romance), consumerism ("whoever amasses the most [expensive, conspicuous] toys, and fouls the environment the most

in furtherance of power, wealth and self-aggrandize-
ment, wins), extroversion (being outer-directed and
dynamic, decisive—a "man of action" in the outer world
(rather than inner-directed and more contemplative:
"passive" = "weak"). It is often the case, for male anger
and rage addicts, that they hold very deep reservations
about whether they "make the grade" as a "man."

The Self-Pact introduces a whole new dimension to
what manhood—"being a man"—may be. There are signs
that this dimension, once felt and embraced, calls into
question any collective, lower-common-denominator
criteria for what it is to "be a man." This new dimension
is personal, unique, and self-affirming.

It is simply this: *"Manhood" comes to be affirmed by the
process of finding, and living out, the very courage it takes
to embark on the Self-Pact commitment and to follow, as
unwaveringly as possible, the adventures of self-discovery
that ensue from "riding the energy of anger and rage—the
ENERGY!!—inwards."* There is a personal conviction
that comes into the foreground through the Self-Pact
commitment that in unhooking from creating victims in
the outer world via triggering and consequent anger and
rage binges, and in daring to risk inner journeys via the
Self-Pact (made possible not because they are not intrin-
sically daunting, but because the sure, outer-world consequences of failing to do so are too horrible to continue

to encounter and live out), one has met some mysterious, yet tangibly felt, internal standard for what it is to "be a man"—at its fundaments, *a principle of one's own very being*. This validation is conferred on oneself, *by oneself*. It is utterly freed from the tyranny of, and therefore independent of, collective images and cultural stereotypes of "maleness." In finding one's true "maleness," one is liberated from the collective.

For women anger and rage addicts—no less at the mercy of collective values and the socialization of gender role stereotyping in terms of identity formation than are men—Self-Pact enactment seems to lead, notwithstanding gender difference, to equivalent—if not exactly the same—results. Quite possibly, the central issue for women differs from that of men. Security of gender-based identity is perhaps less key for women, while *security of personhood* may be more fundamentally at stake. The tyranny of "fashion" (the game of "Who can conform the fastest?") and appearance ("How do I align myself with society's—especially *men's*—values and expectations regarding physical, sexual, attention-garnering attributes, style and demeanor?"), start to give way to a sense of *personhood*—again, *conferred on oneself by oneself*. Wholesale, lowest-common-denominator values around being a "woman" (maybe, if you were raised further up on the food chain, termed being a "lady") and, in terms of men (if this is where one's gender preference as to partner resides), being in competition with other women to gain male attention, start to loosen their grip. In lieu of these more common, compulsive demands, strong firm dignity starts to supplant them. Playing into objectification through obsessive concern with "how I must look!" ... "how I must behave!" ... "how I must 'come across!'" ... makes room for the emergence of personal dignity—the *experiential knowing* of "who I am," "what I am," "what I need," and "what I can choose to do without"—and a different attitude and bearing regarding how to be in, and about, the outer world.

Admittedly, for both women and men anger and rage addicts who, in their anger and rage histories have reached a point of sufficient desperation as to make the Self-Pact commitment necessary, it is still too early to know what the longer-term outcomes regarding personal identity will be, and to what they will lead in terms of worldly bearing. But it is not too early to report that, for both women and men, the Self-Pact seems to open the door to the adventure(s) of personal discovery, and reckoning with "personal identity" is a huge piece of this adventure. *This sense of being embarked on an open-ended adventure is a powerful counterweight to the earlier insecurities and desperation that are such visceral components of both the unleashing of anger and rage ENERGY!!, and the daunting prospect of what might happen to a person if s/he actually holds—embodies—this ENERGY!! consciously without unleashing it outwardly.* This sense of adventuring is, at the very least, a vastly different realization of this ENERGY!!'s potential–and such a contrast to the more prosaic, self-and-other-destructive woes of its ceaselessly repetitive past.

What is an anger and rage addict's "correct" relationship with the energy of Anger and Rage Addiction— the ENERGY!!? (Is "healing" even possible? If so, what might "healing" even mean?)

For those of us, women and men–few in number as of yet–who have committed to the Self-Pact, a question that prevails, and may be far too soon to answer, is "What *is* my correct relationship with the energy–ENERGY!!– underlying Anger and Rage Addiction? As we have seen, more traditional approaches to the problem of anger and rage have not, generally speaking, even drawn close to, let alone embraced, the notion that Anger and Rage Addiction is, at root, an autonomous "energy" (ENERGY!!). Treatment attempts have focused on attempting to control the triggering events, with the aim that they *not* happen, and/or subduing/stifling/snuffing-out/extinguishing the fuse of anger and rage ENERGY!! itself. Along the way, a fair amount of attention has been paid, in the psychotherapy arena, to identifying and dealing with personal "issues" that are seen to be underlying and causative, without much (if any!) appreciation that an addiction process is at work here, in which the "energy"– ENERGY!!–has taken on a life of its own. Under such an unrecognized (and even recognized!) curse, enlightened understanding–insight–are insufficient to counter the suddenness of lightning strikes and their reverberant, thunderous rumbles. Stifling and subduing–attempts to do either or both–are not successful either, because they constitute secular forms of exorcism, and it is incorrect– and likely unconscionable–to try to exile energy–ENERGY!!–that, in its own terms, has a right to be there.

As has become apparent, without any doubt (notwithstanding the small handful of years that the Self-Pact has been in use), at the very least we must acknowledge that the "outcomes" of anger and rage ENERGY!! can run a range from salutary and illuminating, on the one hand, to categorically destructive and toxic, on the other, depending ... Without the Self-Pact in place, The ENERGY!! of Anger and Rage Addiction, proceeding in its "untreated" (or, more likely, inadequately addressed) form is, without exception, destructive and toxic. With the Self-Pact in place, however, during encounters with this ENERGY!!, something new and non-destructive has come into manifestation. As mentioned, it is possible– and even likely–that, given a correct context (as provided by the Self-Pact) it is the very ENERGY!! itself that provides the guidance which leads one towards a fuller, more integrative outcome.

With this new, positive cast as to what the ENERGY!! of anger and rage addiction can, via the Self-Pact, lead, it has already been noted that, at least thus far, the frequency of the triggering events themselves does not seem to have lessened. Triggering incidents have continued to abound! *The overall amelioration of toxic outcomes stemming from trigger-based unleashings is, apparently, an attainment achieved in the presence of ongoing triggering, rather than some kind of benign residue left behind due to any reduction in frequency and emotional intensity of the triggering events themselves.*[9]

Yet the question, "What is my correct relationship with the energy—this ENERGY!!?—still hangs in the air, begging some further, maybe even hopeful, answer. Apparently we are obliged to co-exist with it, but is there no further hope that some sort of less grueling outcome may be possible? We simply don't know, and as has already been stated any number of times about Self-Pact-related outcomes, it may just be too early to know.

So ... in the absence of hard and set experience, regarding what may constitute one's proper relationship

---

9) It is perhaps possible that the frequency of triggering may lessen over the longer term, with the reduction in frequency being too gradual to notice over briefer time intervals. *Maybe* this is the case.

with the ENERGY!! underlying Anger and Rage Addiction (and possibly including all other forms of addiction as well), here is, as least as a start to fathoming this territory, a conjured up list of possible "outcomes" that may stem from consciously engaging it: "exorcism/removal of" the ENERGY!!, "being cleared of" the ENERGY!!, "being relieved of the bondage of" the ENERGY!!, "being restored to sanity regarding" the ENERGY!!, "being helped to 'surrender'" the ENERGY!!, "becoming reconciled with" the ENERGY!!, "learning to coexist (as necessary) with" the ENERGY!!, "healing from" the ENERGY!! (if possible—*whatever* this may mean), "coming to terms with" the ENERGY!! (to good purpose always), "coming into proper alignment with" the ENERGY!!, "coming into proper dis-alignment with" the ENERGY!!, "integrating (with)" the ENERGY!!

Several of the above "outcome" categories: "removing from us," "being relieved of," "being cleared of," "coming into proper dis-alignment[10] with," imply that the ENERGY!! underlying anger and rage addiction, and its triggerings, is somehow foreign, or alien and (therefore) has no rightful place in the mix of qualities which comprise us. This is the attitude, acknowledged or not, of the anger and rage mitigation strategies that have been,

_____

10) "Dis-alignment" means an *intentional* misalignment, or "detuning from," whereas "misalignment" is usually construed as an accidental, unintended occurrence.

prior to the Self-Pact, set forth as representing the "best practices"—state of the art—regarding treatment. If the premise is correct, then ultimately, de facto exorcism or exiling of the ENERGY!! is the final solution. However, one might want to pause for a moment (or longer) to contemplate what the implications of exorcism/exiling, and its lesser cousins suppression and repression, give rise to if they are resorted to—*especially* if the guess about anger and rage ENERGY!!'s having no "rightful place" in our mix is not correct.

Despite its supremely destructive outworkings in its untreated/unaddressed state, underlying Anger and Rage Addiction (along with all other addictions) is, *at its root*—ENERGY!! ENERGY!! = VITALITY!!—the very motive-force of life. Unto itself ENERGY!! is value neutral. It is a resource: a fund that can serve—make possible—life in all its dimensions of being. It—ENERGY!!—infuses everything, and without it there would be no existence.

To exorcise or exile this basic underlying ENERGY!!, even in part, is to remove, at the very least, a portion of the *vitality* that gives life its richness and its endless variation. One doesn't need to be a psychologist to note that people, who, for whatever reason, have managed to squelch—suppress—the expression of emotion (which fuels directly from ENERGY!!), come across as affectively dead, or at least subdued–emotionally constricted and colorless in terms of the "feelings" component of what it is to be human. Loss of vitality is like that. So ... the price of exorcism, as enacted either within a religious or secular (de facto) context, is a high one, indeed. If the ENERGY!! has a rightful place in the mix of who we are, it will never, and shouldn't ever, submit to having its existence denied, or cast aside, like this.

The premise of the Self-Pact, of course, is to "honor" the ENERGY!!'s right to exist, and "be there," and to work with it, and let it work with us, in a more conscious, engaged way.

So, with the price of "exorcism" being such a high one, and apparently not a viable option, where does that leave us regarding healing possibilities that are *inclusive* of the ENERGY!!, rather than "in the absence" of it?

Let's go back to our list of possible outcomes and describe the broader outlines of each one. The first of these is "being relieved of the bondage of." This outcome implies that we are no longer held hostage to, or bound by, or bound up in, destructive consequences of active Anger and Rage Addiction. "Being relieved of the bondage of" does not mean that we are necessarily freed of the burden, but it does mean that we are not tied up in knots by it. If this is an "outcome," we could do worse, for there is a degree of freedom from visiting destructive consequence(s) upon the outer world. And, once again, one is freed-up from a degree of bondage in the presence of the ENERGY!!, not in the absence of it.

"Being restored to sanity regarding" the ENER-GY!!, as an outcome, speaks to the attainment of a certain level of consciousness that can, in some way, remain "sound"–stable–notwithstanding the ENERGY!!'s still being in the mix, (and triggerable). "Sanity"–a legal term (rather than one rooted in the fields of psychiatry and psychology)–can loosely be defined as "soundness of mind." It implies the presence of a stabilizing factor that can mediate between seemingly irreconcilable instinctual (usually compulsive, and often addiction-related) drives, and offset, or counterbalance, wildly veering excursions of addiction ENERGY!!

"Surrendering," as an "outcome," has two facets. The first is the acceptance, usually born of desperation, that, on the basis of one's own unaided resources, one is powerless over addiction ENERGY!! when it is rocking, rolling and roiling our neurology. The second facet of surrender, however, is more far-reaching. Surrender, in this deeper sense, is a recognition and acknowledgement and acceptance of the fact of being afflicted in such ways that, taken all-of-a-piece, is something which constitutes a steady-state, or chronic affliction. *As such, this surrender, in its larger sense, becomes "surrender to (my) life as a human being"—as a being afflicted with a chronic condition replete with acute manifestations—as a* given *to my life, which I must learn to adapt to in some constructive way, or perish.*

In this sense, the outcome of "reconciling with" the presence of addiction ENERGY!! is not unrelated to acceptance. There is, however, one difference. If surrender is an encompassing of the facts, and facets, of personal powerlessness, "reconciling" suggests a greater level of active engagement with the ENERGY!!—becoming "reconciled," as in finding some basis of inner harmony as might arise from "making one's peace with" the need to live "in relation to" this ENERGY!!, rather than categorically despising the ENERGY!!, and oneself for having it.

"Coexist with" as an outcome is also not unrelated to the previous two outcomes ("surrender" and "reconciling"). However "coexisting" highlights the presence of addiction ENERGY!! as a rightful reality. This ENERGY!! has a right to be there and is otherwise immovable. *Any possibility, or hope, for a nontoxic outcome to Anger and Rage Addiction is to be found in full acceptance of the ENERGY!!'s presence and right to exist—right to be (t)here—combined with a conscious taking up of the responsibility to be willing to go to any lengths—to live to good purpose—in the very presence of this ENERGY!!*
If "exorcism" (were it possible and appropriate) consti-

tutes a categorical removal of the ENERGY!!, in which one might live, thereafter, in a liberated, freed state requiring little if any ongoing work to maintain, the "coexist" possibility designates a radically different outcome: knowingly coexisting with an ENERGY!! that continues to be replete with destructive potential, and which wants to be engaged in a highly conscious, even co-operative way if such tragedy is not to come to pass. One may be, in the long run, liberated from negative consequences, but not from the presence—and pressure—of the ENERGY!! itself. This remains one's challenge to deal with.

"Come to terms with—to good purpose always" as an outcome is an extension of acceptance as to the fuller ramifications of "coexistence." Here, however, "co-existence" is ramped up by the exercising of personal resolve. The Self-Pact, in its initial impact on the behavioral repertoire of every anger and rage addict, can be likened to establishing a beach-head in extremely fortified territory. Consciousness—awareness—"storms ashore" and finds itself instantly confronted with, and caught in, a cross-fire of intrapsychic weaponry, and no survival seems possible. To "come to terms with, to good purpose always" can mean many things to many people in their individual particularities of such circumstances. First, it can mean pure, unalloyed determination: "I'm on this beach, picking my way through a minefield, strafed

Stephen Rich Merriman

by machine gun fire, with mortar rounds falling haphaz-
ardly all around me, any one of which could cut me down
or blow me up. I am keenly aware that I may not survive
this, but, *come what may, I am determined not to be driven
back into the sea again.*" In other words, "I'm dealing here
with matters of life and death, and in my resolve to 'not be
driven back into the sea,' I recognize that there are outcomes—in terms of personal dignity, respect and (even) a
sense of personal honor and heroism, that are more important than 'whether I survive this.'" Second, "coming
to terms with—to good purpose always" speaks of what
may be—or become—possible once my "beachhead" has
become more securely established. Are any lines of com-
munication open with my apparent enemy? Do there exist any bases for mutually beneficial accommodations or
exchanges between us? (Even during the horrific trench
warfare of World War I, opposing sides would establish
intervals of truce [truth?] during which soccer [European
football] matches would be played outside the trenches
in temporarily "neutral" territory.) Third, is there anything my apparent enemy has to—and maybe needs to—
teach me/show me about him/her or me? Forth, is there
anything my apparent enemy holds by way of curiosity or
interest about me, areas in which I may have something
to share with him or her that might be mutually useful of
beneficial?

A few words on "coming into proper alignment with" vs.
"coming into proper dis-alignment with" Addiction Energy

The third- and second-to-last entries on the list of possible outcomes are "come into proper alignment with," and "come into proper dis-alignment with" the ENERGY!! Lets take the latter one first.[11]

"Coming into dis-alignment with" leaves open the possibility (seen as unlikely) that the energy of Anger and Rage Addiction—the ENERGY!!—really is sourced in a domain that is sufficiently removed from the centrality of our own being as to be considered an alien force. If this turns out to be so, then those of us with Anger and Rage Addition are its victims, and we are in states of possession as promulgated by this alien energy. In effect, we are, wittingly or unwittingly, hosts to this energy. If this is actually the case, one approach consistent with the exorcism view generally is to counter a state of possession by acting/behaving in ways that render one a progressively less hospitable host to this alien energy. So the theory goes, if one can be consistent with doing this—consciously "dis-aligning," or detuning, from this energy, i.e., behaving in ways that are dissonant to alien energy's intention—sooner or later the energy will take leave, seeking a more suitable, less troublesome host elsewhere.

---

11) Please consult footnote 10, p. 88, which addresses "dis-alignment," vs. "misalignment."

Since no one—current company included—can know all the answers regarding all the vagaries of whatever is capable of bedeviling the human condition, it is only proper that this aspect of "outcome" continue to be included on the list. On the strictly behavioral plane, there is much to commend such an approach.

By contrast, "coming into proper alignment with" is consonant with much of the approach of this monograph, especially the Self-Pact, and is, therefore, consistent with many of the possible outcomes listed and discussed. "Coming into proper alignment with" the ENERGY!! means making relating to this energy—ENERGY!!—an increasingly conscious and ongoing (if laborious) process. The ENERGY!!'s presence, as oft stated, is taken as a given, and a rightful one, at that. "Proper alignment" can be seen as the ongoing refining of one's *relationship* with this energy—ENERGY!!—involving mutual benefit accruing, over time, both to oneself and the ENERGY!! Tall order, that, but maybe it's what we're left with.

Regarding one's "ultimate" relationship with ENERGY!!

We now come to the question of one's ultimate relationship with the ENERGY!! itself. Recall that, beneath the pathology and destructive outworkings of Anger and Rage Addiction is, as so many times mentioned, ENERGY!!. This energy—ENERGY!!—unto itself, is simply raw, and of neutral moral and ethical valence. One might postulate (or, perhaps more humbly, conjecture), as we have done, that this ENERGY!! is, at its fundaments, "vitality"–the very "life" of life–perhaps the primordial (instinctual?) demiurge to exist at all. We've already stressed that if Anger and Rage Addiction could be subdued, or brought under control by the elimination or suppression of this ENERGY!!, there is a huge price to pay in terms of loss of vitality: the constriction of one's emotional life. Richness–breadth of emotional repertoire and experience–is sacrificed. One's ability, for instance, to experience "loss" through immunizing oneself against feeling strong emotion also costs a person their ability to experience joy, and so on.

Thus far in our look at the whole question of Self-Pact outcomes we've, on average, kind of arrived at a sense of how the ENERGY!! of Anger and Rage Addiction, and its destructive potential, are realities that remain in the mix, notwithstanding the fruits of Self-Pact inner adventures. Constant vigilance–sustained and personal exertion on a daily basis–have, thus far, always been necessary to continue to consolidate Self-Pact gains.

Is there no "healing" beyond this?... Or is mutual co-existence (in its various forms) as much as can possibly be expected? (The answer to this question directly addresses the final entry in our "possible outcomes" list on p. 88.)

This is nothing less than the question of what the ultimate possibility is regarding one's relationship with the ENERGY!!–and the vitality it holds. I'll dare (perhaps foolishly) to address this question.

SO ... here goes. Yes, there is, at least in theory, a fuller realization with this ENERGY!! that can be gained– but, thus far, it is only theoretical, and therefore has not, to this point, been realized, nor yet proven to be possible.

Here is the theory presented as succinctly as possible. If (and this is the biggest *"IF"* I can imagine), via the Self-Pact, the destructive outworkings are removed (part of the Self-Pact), and if we, whenever triggered, ride the ENERGY!! of Anger and Rage Addiction inwards–and as we continue to build the muscle to do this repeatedly as triggering continues to occur (continues to play to the expected)–we discover that the ENERGY!! of anger and rage can lead us "inwards" along with it, and reveal things to us, providing us with the underpinnings of experiential "knowings" about things in many dimensions of our being. Clearly, in doing this, the ENERGY!! fueling Anger and Rage Addiction is now showing us that it is capable of constructive awakenings and "acting-ins"–a far cry from reflexive, faster-than-thought acting-outs/ unleashings into, and upon, the outer world.

Hence, the behavioral pathology—anger and rage *unleashing*—starts to be separated out from the ENERGY!! itself. Destructive outworkings of the ENERGY!! still exist as a *potential*, but are no longer, in being triggered, an "actual," or kinetic, destructive reality in the outer world.

As the distinction between the underlying ENERGY!! and its heretofore destructive manifestations becomes clearer, the "ENERGY!!-AS-ENERGY!!—vitality—becomes more clearly recognized, and experienced. (The inner journeying could never occur without it!) *Can this ENERGY!! be increasingly appropriated in a way that reorders the level of its participation with us?—Indeed, can it become* integrated *with us—and we with it—co-present with us, and enriching us, in all life contexts? That is the big question.*

As spectacular as the ENERGY!! of anger and rage appears in its explosive unleashings into the world, that ENERGY!!, in its realization of its own vitality, has, in the past, been truncated and stymied into achieving perverse efficacy only via the bursts and spasms of triggered events. Its flow has never been consistent—has never been a resource to draw us consistently into deeper dimensions of physical, mental, emotional, spiritual, and even mystical, life. Can it now come into our mix as a more constant, unblocked yet still-powerful presence, to deepen our experience of life itself? Can one so en-livened by its vitality, give it—*VITALITY!!*—a wider range of constructive manifestation in our whole personhood? Again, this possibility exists as a theoretical abstraction. Can it be "birthed" into real-world construction and manifestation—into a space-time existence? Hopefully, time, as quite possibly helped along by your own Self-Pact adventures, will tell.

Stephen Rich Merriman

AFTERWORD: THE IRREPRESSIBLE HUMAN PSYCHE

The human psyche is a rich and varied kaleido-scope of consciousnesses. Freud knew it. His simple, elegant formulation of "Id" (instinctual drives, aims and demands), "Superego" (the voice–or maybe intima-tions–of "conscience"–mostly acquired rather than in-nate), and "Ego" (the sense of personal identity trying to mediate–to eke out a middle, livable path notwithstand-ing the oft-opposed, conflictual agendas of Id and Super-ego), grew out of keen observations of unconscious dy-namics, the outworkings of which, in the late nineteenth century, assuming the names of real syndromes such as "neurasthenia," "conversion hysteria," "fugue states," and so on. For Freud, the lineaments of character were "baked in" to the developmental cake by age 5 or so. The rest of one's life would be a series of compromises with, and accommodations to, what had already been set in place.

One of Freud's early disciples, Carl Jung, split with Freud over the depth and range of what the "un-conscious" was up to–and was capable of. For Freud, the Id–libido–was the psyche's mainspring. For Jung, the undercurrents were more nuanced and far-reaching, involving a recognition, and subsequent reconnoitering, of various archetypes residing as potent, active forces in the psyche of each human being, regardless of whether they were acknowledged or not by ego consciousness. An integrative theme of personal wholeness, which Jung termed the process of "individuation," was the goal of personal development—the work of a lifetime. Unlike Freud, who called "Game over!" by the age of 5, individuation, as a lifetime odyssey, could come to fruition only in the second half of life.

Each system of thought—the Freudian (Psychoanalysis) and the Jungian (Analytical Psychology) was rich with observation and alive with dynamism. Freud and Jung were both brilliant observers, and students, of human behavior and consciousness. For each, despite their differences, the psyche was a dynamic interplay of forces that were ever roiling things—with "outcomes" seldom tidy or predictable.

In our era, the dynamic psyche was abandoned to the exigencies and seductive simplifications of reducing human problems to behavioral and biochemical considerations only. "Depth psychology" was discounted as indulgent, fanciful and illusory, and behaviorism, with all attendant behavior modification strategies—along with their touted promise of documentable short-term goals and attainments (and reimbursable, time-limited treatments) came to rule. Get people behaviorally functional, medicalize as pathologies authentic human rights-of-passage experiences such as loss, grieving and other emotional sufferings (for they can be treated with medications to restore "functionality"—no "down-time" necessary!), and deny the dynamics of the human psyche as constituting *intrinsic qualities that need to be encountered on their own terms*. This has been our era in psychiatry, with major spillovers of this influence profoundly affecting psychology, social work and other "helping" professions. The triple tail of "what is modifiable," "what is reimbursable" and "what is treatable with drugs" has come to wag the dog of what should be truly ethical, compassionate, and needed care in service of the *whole* person, inclusive of *soul*.

Behavioral conformity—"functionality"—has increasingly been condoned as something that supplants "having a life"—"my" life, "your" life, with all the individual special-ness, messiness, tissues of meaning and panoply of emotional currents that rightfully comprise, and course within, each one of us.

The dynamic psyche may have been ruled out of existence amidst a climate of efficiency and attendant arrogance characteristic of an overreaching egos-driven, profit-motivated healthcare system, as endorsed by a society that stakes its priority on the god of "functionality," tries to present its studied ignorance as to the true nature of the human condition as some kind of virtue, keeps its eye solely on this laudatory-sounding aim while palms are greased by third-party reimbursability, even as new sub-specialty diagnoses, with special medications at the ready, are promulgated, and incentivized (part of the unseemly history of the "DSM's") in large part by the pharmaceutical industry. The problem, from the standpoint of all these attempts to make human existence conform to simplified models of behavior, abide by "acceptable" societal values, and stay in line via symptomatic treatments, is that the dynamic psyche, the true soul-home of every one of us, has refused to die, or even "play dead." And no amount of behaviorally aimed conformity and drug-induced suppression in furtherance of a standard of "normal functioning" will eliminate it.

It is in the area of Behavioral Addictions—and Addiction generally—that this psychical dynamism is to be once again encountered—as a potential healing agent that no "simple" modification to a behavior and no subduing medication can match. This dynamism of the psyche is an engenderer of a wholeness which is a rightful potential held within the human condition. This kind of intrapyschic healing and wholeness should not ever be abandoned in the compromised interests of societal "conformity," one-dimensional "functionality" and medication-induced numbing.

Throughout this era of behaviorism and drug-facilitated functioning, the dynamic psyche has never been far away—just peremptorily dismissed and ignored. However, given the structural impossibility that behavior modification techniques (in all their varieties) and drug-oriented regimens (nulling out the conjured up "pathologies" of ordinary human experience) can adequately deliver truly human forms of healing, the dynamic human psyche, and depth psychology along with it, roar into the foreground of manifestation once again. *While the Self-Pact was not conceived as an approach out of which depth psychology would receive a new conception—a second birth—it has happened anyway.*

"Riding the ENERGY!!" of anger and rage (and, by inference, any of the troublesome, "triggering" experiences of human life), *inwards*, has revealed what never left: a pluralistic psyche alive with energy, dynamically flowing as it will—capable of both destructiveness *and* healing. This (our) psyche is something that continues to knock on the door, insistent on furthering imperatives to mint more integrative, fully sensate human life: new awarenesses, growth in consciousness and, ultimately, adventures in reconciliation with oneself.

As the Self-Pact continues on to do its work as a healing catalyst in the life of real people wrestling with Anger and Rage Addiction (and, perhaps, with other afflictions of the human soul), so, too, may it confer a dignity on the irrepressibility of the human psyche—ever striving for an increasing attainment of wholeness despite the presence—both within and without—of an array of obstructions and challenges that can appear to make the odds of arriving at wholeness seem very long, indeed.

With the dynamics of the psyche once again revealed, and encountered, experientially, as living forces, however, the odds for realizing reconciliation and wholeness have become "less long" than during the more folly-filled era, now hopefully passing, in which depth psychology and the dynamic psyche were cast aside in pursuit of more short-sighted and less worthy goals.

Such a possibility makes it less daunting, and even, at times (dare I say), genuinely exciting, to greet, each morning, the new dawn.

About the author

Stephen Rich Merriman, living in life's "later innings," devotes his time to family, and other worthy endeavors. Semi-retirement has permitted him to peer out from under the professional "Ph.D.," "psychotherapist" veneer a bit, emboldening him, as a fellow traveler, to write books that seek to prod, and possibly inspire, fuller revealings of humanness on the part of those who read them. He sees all his activities, including educating, teaching, training, and a renewed (very old) career as jazz pianist/composer, as constituting forms of secular ministry. He and his family live, work, and play in the Pioneer Valley of Western Massachusetts.

CPSIA information can be obtained at www.ICGtesting.com
Printed in the USA
BVOW08s0442020615

402346BV00003B/6/P